SPELLING LINKS

Reflections

on spelling

and its place

in the

curriculum

EDITED BY

DAVID BOOTH

Pembroke Publishers Limited

For Carol Fordyce

Acknowledgements
I want to express my gratitude to Ruth Scott and Doreen Scott-Dunne for five years of training in spelling.

— D.B.

© 1991Pembroke Publishers Limited
528 Hood Road
Markham, Ontario
L3R 3K9

Canadian Cataloguing in Publication Data

Main entry under title:

Spelling links

Includes bibliographical references.
ISBN 0-921217-69-2

1. English language – Orthography and spelling –
Study and teaching (Elementary). I. Booth, David.

LB1574.S64 1991   372.6'32'044   C91-094855-0

Editor: David Kilgour
Design: John Zehethofer
Typesetting: Jay Tee Graphics Ltd.

Printed and bound in Canada
9 8 7 6 5 4 3 21

Contents

Introduction

It is a damn poor mind indeed which can't
think of at least two ways to spell any word.
— Andrew Jackson, 1833

When writing I have learned to leave the print representation of words for the moment and to go on putting down my ideas, returning later to worry over the spelling and to seek help from friends and print resources. But for many people, especially children, spelling is such a great problem that they avoid writing, use simple words, take far too long pondering, or give up caring in frustration. Almost everyone I meet apologizes for his or her lack of spelling strengths, and yet I live in a world of academics, writers, and publishers! What lies behind our difficulties with spelling much of the English language, and what attitudes and disabilities are we passing on to our students? We seem to have reached an impasse in our methods of even discussing spelling, with teachers and parents at loggerheads over expectations, with children either being drilled or ignored as developing spellers. Teachers have actually said to me: "I teach spelling, but please don't tell the consultant because we're not supposed to."

As always in education, any change is suspect. The agents of change become martyrs in their missions, or those to be changed resist through fear or ignorance or stubbornness, and the children wander wearily through years of language arts, never knowing what will be expected of their spelling from year to year, constantly asking the question, to no one in particular, "Does spelling count?"

Well, of course it counts, but not as a grade on a paper. In the past, many teachers, myself included, taught spelling as a testing process, with no regard for the experiential and developmental backgrounds of the different children who would be writing the same word. Punishment and humiliation were the order of the day. Poor spellers received zeroes on their papers every Friday for eight years, seldom garnering any strategies or techniques for becoming independent writers. Words were circled, usually in red, with the strange number of four being deducted for each misspelling from the total of twenty-five. Teachers stuck to their principles, and principals would even dictate the words over the public address system, enthralled with their power to instil the fear of writing down a single little word in English. Parents would panic over the test scores and replace reading time at home with drill time for spelling. The cycle never altered year to year, grade to grade.

When I asked a colleague why she publicly displayed the spelling grades on the wall throughout the year, her answer echoed the refrains of moralistic, sinful retribution for "lack of effort". She felt all children could spell all words if only they worked hard enough. She completely disregarded age, competence, background, context, and development. She ruled by the test and rewarded with the chart. This teacher had never read a paper on spelling (never mind a book on language development in children), on the history of the teaching of spelling, on the feelings and attitudes of children being taught spelling, on the development of the spelling text. Her teaching knowledge and practice were based solely on how she had been taught, or even sadder, on how she thought she had been taught.

Is there a teacher among us who did not begin a career by emulating those memories of control at the front of the classroom? And were our images clouded by our insecurities or inabilities to achieve those expected states of perfection? Were we struggling to have, at the very least, a chance to redeem ourselves, to prove our worth by pouncing upon the tiniest error of a child who was trying to make sense of our complex code? I am certain that this was what I did. I taught from a speller, 9:20 a.m. to 9:40 a.m., each and every day, and I tested words on Friday, circled them on Saturday, and returned them on Monday. A meaningless ritual, and I felt competent and righteous. I was nineteen.

What changes us as teachers? What alters our perceptions of what we are trying to achieve with children? When a consultant mentioned to me that spelling was a visual problem, that we try to see each word in our minds, I was instantly aware of the problem with the venerated spelling bee. Why didn't we let children write the words down? Every one of us knows that is exactly what we do when we are asked to spell a word. We have to see it, change it, look at it, match the patterns we have built up over our reading/writing lives. But did we give those children who couldn't spell a buddy, a partner, a group, to collaborate to battle those demons of orthography, so that they too could be part of the meaning-making process?

Nothing I meet in education seems to cause more grief than spelling, even in the 1990s, with computer spell checks, spelling machines, and invented spelling. If I address parents, you can rest assured that, no matter the topic, spelling concerns will be at the top of their list of questions. They are honestly concerned, full of past resentments, present frustrations, and future fears for their children. And like all questions relating to children, these ones cannot be answered simply. For there is no program, no book, no speller, no machine that alone will build language competence in a child. Unfortunately, spelling can't be isolated from other language processes, from attitudes to reading and writing, from homes where print power is seen as valuable, from classrooms where words are recognized as treasures, and where teachers act as guides to that wealth rather than wardens who keep it for themselves. Children trained for a decade in negative spelling teaching have little hope of recovering; there is small chance of their becoming "wordstruck," lovers of language, writers eager and anxious to find and try new words to make subtle meanings, to paint their images with print.

Spelling in English is a complex act, representing hundreds of years, dozens of languages, decades of changes. Those adults who use words, who write frequently, who have facility in spelling, are the very ones who surround themselves with dictionaries of all types, style and structure books, lists, and thesauri, who use mnemonics for those weird words, who notice origins and derivations, who read newspaper columns on contemporary word use, who are not afraid of poems, who can do cryptic crosswords, who engage in word play. And those who failed the spelling tests seldom know the tricks, the support texts, the techniques for spelling. We fail them all the way to the grave.

I worry about authorities who tell us that computers will spell for us, that secretaries will edit our writing, that we will have no need of spelling. Of course they are reacting against the years of torment and failure that so many students have had to endure in the name of learning to spell, and I, too, want to wipe that from the classroom slate. But the spelling of a word *is* a special thing. It is a record of the origins of our language, a recognition of a symbol system that has grown over centuries, so that we can communicate to each other not only ideas, but the history behind those ideas, along with the medium of idea exchange. As we learn about words, we are making thoughtful connections, careful decisions, contributions to sharing.

My son uses a speller in grade four — a traditional, old speller — and he has a weekly pre-test and final test. When we talk about his miscues, he treats them as jigsaw puzzles not yet complete, but he is ready to have a go. There is no fear, no humiliation. His teacher works with words as he does with everything — with energy, commitment, love. He may play the cello while my son works with the word list, and somehow that classroom situation is context enough for learning. I delight in Jay's spelling attempts, his anger over words that shouldn't be spelled that way, his joy over succeeding in approximating a new word. Jay loves puns and riddles and songs and reading and games and commercials. He is word-conscious. He is wordstruck. The speller doesn't seem to hurt in this context.

How Should We Teach Spelling?

Can we teach spelling instruction in a humane, meaningful, and pedagogically sound manner? Can we become informed teachers whose teaching practice is built on a wide background of solid professional research and information? Do most of us teach the way we were taught, believing that God chose the words on the spelling list, and that only drill and pain and repetition will assist us in developing children as spellers? We are certainly not all created equal when it comes to spelling, but the red pen, the marks, the spelling bee, the work books, and the test scores spare no one. Many children have learned to be afraid of words, of reading them aloud, of writing them down, of using them in stories. As teachers we should rejoice in their attempts to master their code, celebrating their humble efforts, building on the beginning patterns of understanding print processes, and collaborating with the children as they develop as language users. We learn to spell by hypothesizing about words, testing our letter memory, confirming and modifying our initial attempts. We know that spelling is a complex cognitive act, that it is a developmental process, that negative feedback on our attempts to invent spellings tells us that we can't learn to spell. When children (and adults) are writing, focusing on spelling correctness during the composing stage will limit ideas and thwart the act of composing. First-draft perfect spelling is an oxymoron for most people.

A very present danger in confronting the difficulties of teaching spelling is that we will give up in despair and retreat from helping children, using such defences as: "You can't teach children to spell — either they are spellers or they are not"; "My jurisdiction has forbidden spelling books, and if they don't care, I don't care"; or "Why bother, when they will all use spell-checks on their computers when they need to spell a word?" I am as guilty of these thoughts as any teacher. When, as a young language arts consultant, I ran a workshop on spelling, I received a call the following day from the principal of one of the teachers in attendance, complaining about that teacher's actions, which he felt had been motivated by my words. I had suggested, imprudently, that we as educators *should throw spellers out the window*, and that is exactly what the young teacher had his students do. The parents complained, the principal reacted, and I had to explain my comments. Perhaps the young teacher was making a point, or mocking my ideas, or rebelling against the principal; I really don't know. But in California, when they banned spelling texts, that story from my youth came floating back, and I realize that now I want to find all the books I can about spelling, including those damnable spellers. Inside their pages we can find information about words, buried beneath boring drill, but there nevertheless. The children, alongside the teacher, can ferret the useful bits out, build their own reference points for learning to spell, make games and puzzles that draw attention to how words work.

My class of student teachers this year were vocal in their descriptions of themselves as poor spellers, and unaware of any strategies or techniques for helping themselves (or their children) become better spellers. What an opportunity we have for developing young teachers as spelling mentors, for releasing into the schools adults who are equipped with background and strategies for promoting word awareness. We will never know how to spell all words. We will never know all about all words. We will continue to grow as language learners all our lives. Spelling is not over in grade six. It should not just be corrected by secondary school teachers; it should be taught, through writing, through poetry, through puzzles and games, through reading, through discussion and debate about words, through linguistic exploration, through second languages, through reference helps, through modeling by effective and affective teachers.

Gold stars are no reward for spelling work. They are marks of praise for short-term memory by those students who play the game. I want my child to be instructed in spelling, to be taught, helped, enabled, informed, enriched by teachers who care about the whole of language, who consider spelling one of the components in developing "print power". As a young teacher, I used reward and punishment, humiliation and praise, tests and homework, shame and blame, to teach spelling. I was absolutely ignorant of research and development in the teaching of spelling. I was a Dickensian archetype until I met language arts consultant Bill Moore, who opened up to me the riches of teaching and learning about words all the time, not for only twenty minutes each morning, but every time my class and I read or wrote, every time we sang or played, every time we laughed at a joke. He taught us to question and challenge why words work as they do, to learn about their origins, to laugh at their incongruities, to marvel at their complexities and wonder at their power. He was the finest of spelling teachers, and he never mentioned the subject of spelling during those years.

I like Winnie-the-Pooh's attitude to spelling: "My spelling is Wobbly. It's good spelling but it Wobbles, and the letters get in the wrong places."

Rethinking Our Spelling Programs

Perhaps our problem in teaching spelling lies not in the argument about which words to choose to teach but in our lack of understanding of *how* children learn to spell and our unrealistic expectations of children. Spelling is a complex cognitive process learned over time, and bound in with all the other language experiences that change us — the books we read, the stories we tell, the friends we know. Spelling is part of the whole of language, and while we may ask children to focus for the moment on one aspect, we must always remind ourselves to connect that part to the whole of language, so that patterns and information sink into our children's long-term memories.

In my own teaching, I have come to accept that mastering spelling is a forever process, a life skill. Knowledgeable and dedicated teachers can help children cope with the difficulties of spelling and see the spelling of words as a window to the history of our language; they can open up to them the joy that can be found in the interplay of letters and sounds found in the words that make us human.

Fortunately, in the last while, many researchers, educators, and teachers have been developing programs to assist us in actually teaching spelling in a meaningful and significant manner, giving us the background and ideas we need to implement a spelling curriculum within a holistic approach to language.

I have asked the contributors to this book to help me grow in spelling lore, to add to my teaching theory and background, to take me beyond my beginnings as a spelling teacher thirty-five years ago. I want to know that those learning to teach today (and those, like myself, who are relearning) will have a basis for developing a language program that truly incorporates spelling, neither shutting it out nor focusing on it as the heart of literacy, but seeing it as what it is, a way of encoding meaning, of writing what you mean, in careful, concise, exact terms.

The contributors whose work appears here do not all agree with each other. (They don't even agree about the spelling of specific words: some write *colour* and *centre*, others *color* and *center*, reflecting the spelling systems they learned in their own childhoods.) You should pick and choose the ideas and suggestions that will work best for your students' needs right now.

When you help a child spell a word that connects linguistically to other words in his/her world, you open up the power of language. That child is learning to give shape to his/her own thoughts on the page, without fear of spelling a particular word, but rejoicing in knowing that one pattern leads to others, and finally to control of writing. The child who is learning to spell comes to realize that the more he/she knows about language, the more empowerment he/she has in making meaning, in communicating with others.

David Booth
Toronto
July 1991

PART I

The Nature of Spelling

Benjamin Franklin, among others, attempted to reform the alphabet for English by adding six new letters, to make our written language more phonetic, and to help those of us who are poor spellers. There would be no more silent letters to perplex us; each letter would represent a single sound.

Fortunately, or unfortunately, traditional spelling patterns have on the whole remained the same, and we as teachers are still left trying to find our way through this complicated maze.

Rosemary Courtney takes us back in time for a look at the beginnings of English language spelling, and offers some astute reflections on the implications for today's teaching.

A Spelling History
Dr. Rosemary Courtney

Reasons for Teaching Spelling

English spelling is seen as both difficult and necessary, and therefore important to teach. Unlike languages such as Italian or even German, which have a perfect or highly consistent relationship between sound and letter, the English language does not have a one-to-one phoneme-grapheme correspondence. Vowel sounds in particular can be spelled in a bewildering variety of ways, largely for historical reasons, which are illogical to the present-day student.

The English student, then, has to pay attention to spelling, while his less burdened Italian counterpart never gives it a moment's thought. Moreover, in the English-speaking world, "correct" spelling has acquired over many years a cultural or social value out of proportion to its practical use, namely to ease communication. A misspelled article, however fluent, valid, and sophisticated, will be regarded as "illiterate" on the basis of its spellings alone, which will outweigh its literary or other merits. An ability to spell is regarded as almost equivalent to moral virtue; people who find spelling difficult — that is to say, most people — are usually "ashamed" of this "fault" while cheerfully acknowledging illegible handwriting, ignorance of the use of the semi-colon, or confusion between similar words. "I'm no good at English, I can't spell" is a statement heard from young and old, naive and sophisticated alike.

There is no question of the value which our society places upon "correct" spelling, for reasons good or ill. And conformity to all the values of society is still assumed to be the prime purpose of education. Teachers therefore feel obliged to equip their students with this deemed necessity. In so doing, they are faced with bewildering alternatives, between integrated programs and spelling programs as such, between phonic methods and visual methods, between one publisher's word lists and another's. They do not have the time to evaluate for themselves even the few different programs which their regional board approves. This paper examines some of the practices, past and present, which shape the way we think of spelling and the teaching of it.

The Idea of Correct Spelling

The present system of English orthography, like the language itself, is the result of organic growth rather than academically determined development.

Until at least the seventeenth century there was no such thing as "correct" spelling. Manuscript scribes and then printers spelled words as they thought best, according to their own dialects, traditions, and tastes. The invention of printing, far from stabilizing spelling, introduced more variety into an orthography which had been reaching an agreed standard in the hands of trained professional scriveners: printers (often self-educated artisans rather than learned scholars) often chose a spelling which would enable the type, for want of machine justification, to fill out a line to the right margin and in early years had to employ English compositors with imperfect knowledge of English. When English compositors were trained, their individual spellings, even while internally consistent, diverged one from the other, so that a large book such as Shakespeare's First Folio, which needed five different people to set the type, could show as many as five different spellings of any one word. The fact that internal orthographic consistency was less usual among private writers than among printers is instanced by three extent signatures of Shakespeare, which are all differently spelled.

Gradually, though, through the fifteenth and sixteenth centuries, printers at least came to adopt a more uniform set of spellings. Many of these spellings, which have since passed into modern times, were based on earlier transcriptions which were themselves faulty, owing their form to scrambling of dialects, to mis-hearing by a foreign scribe, to calligraphic convention, to wrongly supposed classical etymology, or to arbitrary distinction. Nevertheless, the habit of spelling certain words in a certain manner had already taken hold by the time Elizabeth I came to the throne. Soon the more professional master printers established their house styles. While not identical — house styles to this day vary, even within the same country, from publisher to publisher and from newspaper to newspaper — these orthographies had a remarkably high level of agreement. It remained only for some self-styled authority to codify the existing system to spread printers' usage into private practice.

This task was inevitably undertaken by teachers. Two in particular, fired with the intellectual enthusiasm of the English Renaissance, addressed themselves to the learned and to the tradespeople respectively. Richard Mulcaster, a conservative, chose to advocate traditional spellings confounded by the fashion for classical learning, while Edmond Coote produced spelling books for the lower middle class in which frequency of usage dictated selection. Since there was already a large measure of agreement on the forms of most words, the two books conflicted rarely, and their immense popularity and widespread distribution over more than a century ensured universal acceptance of the orthography of the time. Finally, Samuel Johnson's seminal *Dictionary of the English Language*, published in 1755, provided the needed handy reference work indispensable to private writers up to Victorian times. He did not, as is commonly supposed, determine spelling, but as a true lexicographer, simply recorded it, giving common usage the weight of his personal authority and the added benefit of his style — even when, by his own admission, he was wrong. Johnson's spellings are more or less the same as are generally accepted today, apart from such details as the final *k* in *musick*. English spelling was therefore standardized in practice and fixed in the *Dictionary* by the middle of the eighteenth century. Almost two and a half centuries later, pronunciation has changed but spelling remains the same, thus accounting for some of the apparent discrepancies between orthography and phonemes.

A subsequent lexicographer on the other side of the Atlantic was, however, personally responsible for several changes in spelling which have become standard American usage. Noah Webster's first publication, a scant thirty years after Johnson's *Dictionary*, adopted Johnson's spellings (including *honour*); only six years later he advocated spelling reform, enshrining a selection of his proposed changes in his own dictionary (including *honor*). Like Johnson, he recorded spellings already used; but unlike Johnson, he chose from the available alternatives the form he personally preferred, for orthographic or even for merely nationalistic reasons. Webster's "authority" established itself by default, for lack of widely disseminated competition. But the effect of this authority to the present day is evidenced by the proliferation of "Webster's" dictionaries — good, bad, and indifferent — permitted by the copyright laws which denied to his original publishers, G. and C. Merriam, the sole rights to his name.

In the minds of the public, then, there really is such a thing as the "correct" way to spell a word, although what they really mean is a form agreed in the particular country (Canadian spelling being divided between that of Britain and the United States). Scriveners devised it, printers agreed to it, lexicographers recorded it. The "authority" is that of history and tradition, backed by the strictures of many generations of schoolteachers.

Those who value history and tradition less than phonetic logic have long argued for spelling to be made more consistent with pronunciation, and have devised many diverse schemes for representing English sounds. But the spelling reform movement, while still active, is no nearer achieving its aim than it was four hundred years ago. That being the case, children will continue to have to struggle with the orthographic system which presently obtains, with all its irregularities and pitfalls.

This difficulty is in some cases confounded by the lack of stability of the system itself: children can accept the notion of "correct" spelling, however false, and can learn which alternative is desired; where the system itself admits of more than one acceptable form, their sense of security may be threatened and doubts arise as to the reality of correctness itself. This is particularly the case in Canada, where many words may be spelled either one way (usually British) or another (usually American). Consistency in one or other of these systems is not even expected, so that a child can defend the use of *color* in one context and *centre* in another. A system of divided usage being itself unsystematic, it is little wonder that children are notoriously careless about the accuracy of their spelling. They lack the rigid notion of "correctness" which obtained in England during centuries of mechanistic education, with its emphasis on the detailed structure of Latin.

In default of a true "correctness" in spelling on either side of the Atlantic, there exists a set of agreed-on spellings with a limited number of alternatives. Until the spelling reform people have their way (and can agree on a system, which seems unlikely in view of the divergence of pronunciation in space and time), children need to be equipped with a method or methods of producing spellings acceptable to their teachers and their readers.

Possible methods of teaching spelling are also the subject of endless argument; they are based on certain assumptions which change as new evidence is brought forward, sometimes without a careful examination of the evidence itself. For example, a phonetic (or more properly, phonemic) approach to spelling is based largely on new "evidence" that English spelling is more regular than was once supposed. This conclusion is debatable and has been exaggerated in the public mind. If English spelling is phonemically consistent, why has it always proved so difficult to learn?

Why English Spelling Is Difficult

The difficulties of English spelling, as Alice Watson pointed out in 1935, lie both in the words themselves and in the person trying to spell them. Difficulties in the words are phonemic: the alphabetic system prompts expectation that it will represent the sounds of the language in a one-to-one relationship. A non-alphabetic writing system, such as Chinese, gives rise to no such expectation. English confuses its writers precisely because it is partly phonemic, but not wholly so. How much of the orthopgraphy is phonemic, with one symbol for one sound and one sound always represented by the same symbol, has recently become a matter of debate, after at least four centuries of complaint about its inconsistencies.

The very fact that difficulties in mastering English spelling (probably the root of its exaggerated social value) have persisted for so many years should be proof enough that our system of orthography is largely inconsistent with any form of pronunciation. Yet two major modern studies have attempted to show a large measure of regularity, with untoward consequences in curriculum design.

Paul Hanna, an American structuralist, has long held that the system of English spelling is basically phonemic. In a study produced in 1953, he and his student James Moore claimed that 80 percent of English phonemes were regularly spelled in a certain way. Challenged on the grounds of inadequate data (a word list comprising only 3,000 words), separate classification of "silent" letters, and treatment of unstressed vowels before *r* as a unit, he undertook, in 1963, an extensive computer-assisted study with U.S. government funding. The computer was programmed to match the phonemes in any word with their possible orthographic realizations, according to a detailed algorithm of patterns; the corpus this time comprised more than 17,000 words from the Merriam-Webster *New Collegiate Dictionary* (sixth edition), which also supplied the style of phonemic transcription. The matching was then analysed.

The results of the analysis show that the computer, obeying its given rules almost without error, spelled in the usual manner (i.e., "correctly") 49.87 percent of the words whose phonemes were supplied. Attempting to match his previous claim for an 80-per-cent regularity, Hanna has added to the "correct" total those words which were spelled by the computer with "only one error" (a further 36.4 percent), producing an impressive total of 86.27 percent of words spelled "correctly or almost correctly". These figures he claims as a high phoneme-grapheme correspondence.

I have four objections to this claim. In the first place, the only true figure is the 49.87 percent of words which the computer spelled without error: many a child being penalized for spelling mistakes could justifiably plead that many of his or her misspelled words contained "only one error"; but the criterion in spelling is absolute, not relative accuracy — a child is required to spell correctly, not "almost correctly". English spelling is therefore, even by this computer analysis, at best only half regular. It is the other half that causes the problems.

In the second place, the phonemic representation of many words is phonetically unsound: the pattern input to the computer does not always resemble the usual pronounciation of the word. This is only partly the fault of the source dictionary, which gives alternate pronunciations, including but not only the kind chosen for use in this study. The phonemic analysis of any given word is more that of an exaggeratedly careful pronunciation such as is possible only when reading the word from its spelling, not when spelling the word from its sound. This careful pronunciation uses, in particular, the strong form of the unstressed vowel, whereas a child saying the word in the only way he or she knows, would have no means of reconstituting the unknown vowel. For example, the phonemic input to the computer of the following words is not a transcription of any normal pronunciation, least of all that of an American whose speech it is supposed to represent:

problem / problɛm /
compensation / kompɛnseʃən /
library / laibrəri /
sacrilegious / sækrilidʒəs /
temporarily / tɛmpowrɛrəli /
rehearsal / rihɛrsæl /
propeller / propɛlər /
ocean / owʃæn /
program / prowgræm /

The word *program* in particular is almost a test case of American as distinct from Canadian pronunciation, with its characteristic [ə] (schwa) in the unstressed syllable.

In the third place, the computer can be relied upon to generate spellings in almost total consistency with the rules it has been programmed to follow. Children, however, are not machines and cannot be so programmed. Moreover, the rules of the algorithm are so complex that they are difficult for an adult to read, let alone memorize, even if the vital factor of motivation is ignored. Meanwhile, "regularity" can be defined according to various criteria of how many rules can be expected to be absorbed, and what these rules are.

Lastly, the match between phoneme and grapheme depends upon the phonemic breakdown of words supplied to the computer. A child being asked to spell a word is required to supply his or her own phonemic analysis; and this, as many a teacher of the much easier task of phonic *reading* can testify, is extremely difficult for the average child, even discounting the extra and crucial problem of unstressed vowels.

If the Hanna study were purely linguistic, a theoretical statement of supposed phoneme-grapheme correspondence of technical interest to linguists, my criticism would be based on the first two counts only, which are statistical and phonetic; but since he does draw implications for teaching from his "findings", the latter two pedagogical objections must also be taken into account.

Following the Hanna study came an examination, which *is* purely linguistic, of the sound system of English, necessarily incorporating orthographic considerations. Chomsky and Halle, among their detailed analysis, conclude that "English orthography, despite its often cited inconsistencies, comes close to being an optimal orthographic system for English." This conclusion is based on another assumption, namely that children can, much in the same way that they know without articulating the complex rules of grammar, similarly internalize the "underlying phonological representation" of a word. But Chomsky and Halle are referring more to the mechanisms of *reading*, in which decoding a possible sound from a series of alternative spellings is considerably easier than spelling, in which one has to choose which of the alternatives is acceptable. Moreover, Chomsky and Halle specifically exclude exceptions, which pose the greatest difficulty for beginning or weak spellers.

Unfortunately, the sweeping conclusions of these writers have been taken as authoritative by such influential bodies as the committees that compile curriculum guides for schools. Since English spelling is now thought, albeit on such tenuous evidence, to be far more regular than was previously believed, a return is being advocated to phonic methods of spelling based on auditory perception, which is not necessarily the best or most common technique by which children can learn to spell. Phonic spelling only holds good for half the language, by Hanna's count; as for the rest, it is all very well for him to state that "many of the errors do not constitute serious spelling problems. Many of them would be obviated with the mastery of simple morphological rules." He is implying that spelling is really not all that difficult, and all that is needed is a thorough phonic base; yet he was contradicted earlier by Ernest Horn, who stated:

> It has been suggested that children would be greatly helped by being taught to spell each sound by the commonest spelling. Yet a check of the actual spellings of one fifth grade for an entire year showed that if certain sounds had been uniformly spelled by the commonest spellings, the number of errors would have greatly increased.

The amount of increase, he instanced, ranged from six times to twenty-five times the previous number of errors.

As far as the difficulties arising from the words themselves is concerned, the major factor is the extent of sound-symbol correspondence. It is less of a problem in reading, partly because recognition is so much easier than recall. In reading, a child only needs to make an intelligent guess at a word, using contextual clues to provide a set of alternatives, phonic clues to narrow the choice, and recognition to confirm a known word; in silent reading, an inaccurate but near guess will not interfere with the child's understanding of the text; in oral reading, a reasonable teacher will accept a meaningful substitution as evidence that the child is interacting with the print. But in spelling, the child has to provide the written form of a word from his or her oral/aural vocabulary; the only clues are phonic, and the alternatives, especially for vowel sounds, are numerous. No other help is available, recall of a previously learned form may prove elusive, and yet total accuracy is demanded. As Margaret Peters succinctly expresses the decoding/encoding discrepancy:

> Reading is from the unknown via the context to the known. Spelling is from the known to the unknown.

If English spelling were as regular as Hanna and Chomsky would have us believe, the difficulty of encoding would be minimal, as it is for the Italian child.

Naturally, the problem of regularity, in addition to its definition, varies according to the words which the child chooses or is required to spell. A child writing monosyllabic words of the kind formerly found in basal readers ("Run, Dick, run. . ."), that is, words with predictable phoneme-grapheme correspondence, stands a better chance of producing an acceptable spelling than one who tries to write longer words with unstressed vowels and idiosyncratic spellings. The difficulty of spelling increases as less predictable words are added to the child's writing vocabulary, which themselves may confuse existing mastery of easier words. *Then*, for example, becomes confused with *than*, *for* with *four*. This confusion seems to increase with age, presumably as a function of widening vocabulary: the lists of misspelled words from a total population of adults and children do not agree with those from young children, the total population misspelling *more* phonemically regular words.

The supposed regularity of English spelling is not conclusively proved, therefore, by either Hanna or Chomsky. The exact proportion of regularity, by any criterion, being still undetermined, it can be assessed at less than the half proposed by Hanna, possibly around a third. These phonically regular words can be learned by auditory methods, but other words require different or supplementary techniques, together with a reduction of the expectation that written English "should" be alphabetic, as Hanna and Chomsky (and the spelling reformers) seem to think.

In addition to the vexed question of phonemic regularity, words can cause spelling difficulties when their length results in omission of a syllable. Homophones are also a source of misspelling since even when a child has mastered both or all forms, he or she can still remain confused as to which form to write in a given context.

Difficulties arising within the speller vary from perceptual problems of hearing, sight, motor coordination and speech, to the lack of abilities such as field independence, visual imgery, short-term and long-term memory, and analytical thinking. Spelling ability seems to be correlated to a certain extent with general intelligence, and to a greater extent with school experience, verbal ability, and reading. Some people, even with high achievement in other language skills, seem to have a special incapacity for spelling just as others may have a "mathematics block".

Some of this special disability, or even the ordinary struggle with spelling which most people experience, may be due to attitude — on the part of society as represented by the teacher, or on the part of the speller. Society demands such a high standard of spelling, frowning upon even one misspelling in an entire paper, that any such misspelling is disproportionately prominent: teachers and readers alike ignore the high ratio of correct spellings, to focus only on negative production. This

can create in the mind of the uncertain speller an image of himself or herself as a "poor speller", an image difficult to eradi-
cate and crucial to spelling achievement. In addition, since the
poor speller is usually a person who does not value highly such
matters as attention to detail and careful presentation of work,
his or her interest in spelling is usually low. It takes a person
who really loves words and cares about getting them right to
be motivated to spell well, as spelling is not intrinsically
interesting. Motivation being the key to all learning, it is the
vital factor in good spelling: as Peters says, the speller's "attitude to the skill exerts a very great influence on success in it."

All these difficulties in spelling, whether in the words or in
the speller, have been the subject of many research studies, especially in this century. Hanna and Chomsky have attempted to
reduce the difficulty of irregular spellings; other studies, in line
with the modern trend to match teaching methods to children's
learning strategies, have dealt with factors such as perception
and motivation with a view to improve spelling instruction in
the light of proven psychological and pedagogical principles.

The Teaching of Spelling

Any consideration of the teaching of spelling presupposes certain assumptions mentioned previously: that since education
is to bring children into line with society, it is both possible
and desirable to teach spelling; and that there is such a thing
as correct spelling to be taught.

History

In earlier centuries these assumptions were not questioned, and
methods of imparting the desired skill were not properly investigated until the twentieth century. Prior to that, as children
were drilled in reading, handwriting, and computation, so they
were drilled in spelling. A daily list of difficult words (irrele-
vant to the pupils' own writing and often quite useless for adult
life) were provided, pupils were set to commit them to memory, largely by rote and rule, and those who failed to reach the
high standard of (usually oral) spelling in the subsequent test
were punished. There is no record of the success rate of this
mechanistic method, but complaints from teachers and then
employers of the poor spelling of the pupils were as common
then as now — and this in a time before compulsory educa-

tion, when the recipients were pre-selected and educational goals limited.

The only consideration in early spelling instruction was not whether spelling should be taught (it was assumed that it should be) or why it should be taught (seen as axiomatic), but only what should be taught. The literature is concerned solely with the choice of words to be given to the pupils for study. In this century the choice of word lists has come under more elaborate scrutiny as the goals of spelling instruction, as of education in general, have become more clarified and increasingly child-centred. Word lists remain an important topic, but examination of spelling principles has now widened to include consideration of how spelling should be taught.

Methodology is dependent upon principles, which themselves are dependent upon the perceived goals of the instruction. In the nineteenth century the goals were to produce competent clerks capable of producing well-presented copy; spelling instruction for children was therefore geared to teaching the words which were assumed to be needed in adult life. While this consideration remains prominent among present-day goals with varying degrees of emphasis, the highest priority is now being given to those words which children need in their own writing, usually chosen on the basis of representative frequency counts. It is felt that the skills developed in the practice of words meaningful to children will serve them later in learning the spellings of new words. Since one of the skills is that of using a dictionary to locate and check spellings, the development of this skill is seen as an essential component of an effective spelling program. Spelling is also seen as a means to an end, that of producing effective writing, in which vocabulary development plays an important part. The total aim is to develop in children an attitude towards accuracy in spelling words, an attitude which can be transferred from known words to unknown words, and which is closely related to careful presentation of the written material as a whole. Each child should learn to check his or her work carefully, to proofread spelling errors, to correct punctuation, and to write legibly. This is, more or less, how things stand in the early '90s.

PART II

Spelling as a Developmental Process

My son brought his letter to his grandmother to me for assistance, and as I began to read, admonished me to "read it like a father, not an editor." I am filled with terror that in my zeal to provide children with the best linguistic backgrounds I can, I prevent them from writing what they think and feel at a particular growth point in their lives. From watching my son, I know that spelling is a developmental process, and that the strategies I provide for him must be appropriate to his age and stage of growth at the moment. Some children tell time in grade one; he mastered digital and analogue clocks at nine. How students spell is governed by their evolving knowledge about spelling and about how words work.

Jim and Carol Beers are renowned for their spelling research, and in their fascinating article, they carefully describe their findings about the development of spelling in children. J. Richard Gentry offers his own view of this development, and Edmund Henderson and Shane Templeton describe different stages and their implications for teaching.

A Developmental Basis for Spelling Instruction

Dr. Carol S. Beers and Dr. James W. Beers

Many people assume learning to spell is primarily a memorization task. In fact, most people consistently refer to good spellers as having good memories and poor spellers as having poor memories. Certainly, spelling instruction does not take up as much time as writing or reading instruction. So why should we spend time writing about children's spelling? The answer is relatively straightforward for us as teachers. When we begin to examine children's spelling attempts in their writing, we begin to understand what children know about their written language system. Children's spelling attempts are not merely a reflection of memory, but rather a reflection of their understanding and experience with written words.

Let's begin by looking at this piece of writing by a young seven-year-old boy. We will call him Todd.

> I AM A DMDM I AM STPIT FOR REAL I HOEP I JEUT TRT IN TO A CAR. DO YOU WEAT TO NO WHY BE CIS I AM DM. NOW I'LL TELL YOU NOW LETS BEGIN TO THE STAR. I AM CAZE BECIS I AM VERRY CASE THIS IS MY SECAT TIME I DAN TOW MUTAS AND I HATIT EVEN I AM NO VERY GOOD IN READING AND THATS ALL. (I am a dumb dumb. I am stupid for real. I hope I just turn into a car. Do you want to know why? Because I am dumb. Now I'll tell you. Now let's begin at the start. I am so crazy because I am very crazy. This is my second time [repeating first grade]. I've done two mistakes and I hate it. I am not very good in reading and that's all.)

As we examine this child's writing, we might initially see many mistakes. After all, there are many misspelled words, many letters left out of words, and many short and long vowel errors. His writing sounds more like talk than it does writing. We might even consider this child a prime candidate for early remedial help. Todd, however, is only in the first grade and this story was his first extended piece of writing. What does his spelling tell us about his understanding of the written language system? Todd has a good sense of sentence structure; he uses initial and final consonant sounds when spelling; he recognizes word boundaries; and he makes use of the English sound system as he attempts to spell unknown words.

If we look at an example of his later writing, we see much evidence of growth.

> MY FRIENDS ASKED IF I COULD COME TO THE ROLLER SKATING PARTY. MY MOM SAID YES TO THEM. WHEN WE GOT THERE THEY WERE HAVING A BALL. I PUT ON MY ROLLER SKATING SHOES TO GO SKATING. I HAD FUN THERE. AFTER A WHILE, THE PARTY WAS OVER. I ENJOYED THE ROLLER SKATING PARTY. AND THIS WAS ALL.

As we examine Todd's later spelling, we see a dramatic evolution in his ability to use sentence structure, as well as spell vowel sounds and word endings correctly. Dramatic, though not unusual.

We believe it is important to analyse and evaluate children's spelling within their writing attempts so that we can better understand their developing knowledge of written words. Todd's writing raises questions about not only his knowledge of the spelling system, but also other children's knowledge as well. For example, do other children spell as Todd does? Will other children's spelling change as dramatically as Todd's did? Will Todd's (and other children's) spelling attempts continue to tell us about his knowledge of English spelling? And, most importantly, will Todd's spelling attempts suggest possible instructional strategies which can be used to assist him in his growing knowledge of words?

To help answer these questions about children's spelling, we would like to share the results of our research on children's spelling, as well as the research done by others during the past fifteen years. Rather than discuss a series of studies, we will share some of our conclusions from these studies and refer you to Henderson and Beers (1980) and Templeton and Baer (in press) for a more in-depth reading, should you desire. The primary purpose of all of these studies was to try to determine what kinds of errors children made as they spelled and why they made these kinds of errors.

When children write, they do not make random spelling errors. We do know that when children write, their spelling errors are consistent and are similar to the errors found in children's writing in many parts of the country. Children do not just use a random set of letters to spell words but rather systematically pick very specific letters. For example, DG often spells *dog*, KT often spells *cat*, RUNING spells *running*, and SMILLING often spells *smiling*. WE see many examples of fairly consistent spelling errors in the following story by Susan.

> WE WAT UP THE HOLE IT FALT LAKE SAM WAS PELLING ME
> UP THEN WE WAT DONEY THE HOLE IT WAS E SZYER THEN
> WE WAT DONEY THE HOLE BECAUSE GRAVITY WAS PELLING
> ME BACK. (We went up the hole. It felt like some one was
> pulling me up. Then we went down the hole. It was eas-
> ier then. We went down the hole because gravity was pull-
> ing me back.)

In Susan's story we see the common substitution of *a* for *e* in

WAT (*went*) and FALT (*felt*), as well as the omission of the nasal *n* before the final consonant *t* in WAT (*went*). These errors are typical of a young writer and have been found in many children's writing.

Children use their knowledge of written words they know as they attempt to spell words they do not know.
Children's spelling attempts are not merely haphazard guesses with no relationship to other words. For the most part, children make use of words they already know. Thus, we might expect to see a word such as *wake* spelled WACK. After all, *ck* is often used to represent the final / k / sound at the end of words. Or we might see *stick* spelled STIKE. In both instances we see the incorrect application of a common spelling generalization for the / k / sound. The student who overgeneralizes in spelling is common in the primary grades. What is important to remember is that the generalization may be correct, but is applied incorrectly to words which have similar sounds. Children are constantly making connections with what they already know about their written language system as they attempt to write unknown words.

When children learn to spell, this learning occurs developmentally, much as other language learning.
When children begin to write, they do not spell words correctly, just as when they begin to talk, they do not pronounce words correctly. It takes children several years to master all aspects of the oral language system. Learning to spell also takes several years, and occurs developmentally, through several sequential stages. These stages include the prephonetic stage, the early phonetic stage, the phonetic stage, the structural stage, and the meaning/derivational stage.

During the *prephonetic stage*, the child uses letters for words and may even occasionally use numbers for words. This stage, most common during the preschool years, is often characterized by no discernible letter-sound pattern. Letters may be written continuously as in ABDG for *wally* or separated into groups as in CT OEG. Often a child will write a set of letters and ask what word it spells. Generally, words at this stage are not readable as we expect them to be. The following examples were taken from a four-year-old's attempts at writing:

ITITOZ for *house*
XZWQTTT for *cat*
XZWQ for *kitten*

Children may move rapidly into the *early phonetic stage*. The signal for this movement is the presence of a phonetically appropriate letter for a word and phonetic representation for word boundaries. During this stage, children's writing becomes somewhat readable, although context is particularly important in understanding what is written. Initial and final consonants generally appear during this stage, although certain letters are regularly omitted, especially vowels. The following examples of a five-year-old's writing indicates this slightly more advanced stage of spelling:

D D P T D D H S for *Daddy painted the house*
I G T A H R T for *I got a shirt*
A G A B C I G A B S B for *I got a book. I got a baseball.*
I G A K H U N for *I got a key chain*
I GT A KT HM for *I got a cat at home*

In these examples Jamie, the writer, is clearly making sense of the English sound system as he attempts to write words, even though only one letter may be used for a word. His initial and final consonant sounds appear in the last example, as do evidence of word boundaries. His last example in particular becomes more readable to any adult and less dependent upon context for interpretation. All of these examples, however, are more advanced than the four-year-old, who has made no attempt to use letter sound correspondence.

The *phonetic stage* of spelling development generally occurs during the primary school grades. The stage is referred to as the phonetic stage because children tend to use their understanding of how English sounds are produced as they attempt to spell unknown words. During this stage, children gradually develop more control over written words. This control is demonstrated fairly consistently with the consonant letters. Long vowel sounds are represented by the one letter which says that vowel's name. The long vowel *a*, for example, will be represented by the letter *a* without any regard for the second vowel (the vowel marker) necessary. During this period, we might see the word *cake* spelled CAK or the word *bike* spelled BIK.

A second interesting feature of this stage is the child's representation of the short vowel sounds. On the surface, it may appear that the child does not hear the sound correctly and so totally misrepresents the short vowel sound in the word. Thus, the word *bed* might be spelled BAD or *big* might be spelled BEG. These spellings, however, reflect again the child's understanding of how sounds are produced. The letter *a* is often used to represent the short *e* sound because of their similarity in pronunciation. If a child attempts to sound out the short *e* sound, his or her mouth is in a position to also say the name of the letter *a*. The same is true of the letter name *e*, which is often used to represent the short *i* sound. (See Read (1975) for a complete discussion of this phenomenon.) Thus, in Susan's story we see WAT for *went* and in Todd's story we see EVIN for *even*.

Two other features of this stage include the omission of preconsonant nasals and the phonetic spelling of word endings. The preconsonant nasal is the nasal (*m* or *n*) sound that comes before a consonant. In the word *jump*, for example, the *m* is the preconsonant nasal. When children in the phonetic stage spell words with a preconsonant nasal, they often omit that nasal sound. This is not because they do not hear the sound, but because they have an implicit understanding that the subsequent consonant is more important and actually predicts what the preconsonant nasal should be. The *p* in **jump**, for example, can be immediately preceded by *m* but not *n* as part of the same syllable. During this stage, children may spell *jump* as JUP, *long* as LOG, and *went* as WAT because of their focus on the subsequent consonant. Thus, Todd spells *second* as SACAT (omitting the *n*) and Susan spells *went* as WAT (also omitting the *n*).

Lastly, children in this stage may typically represent word endings phonetically. They do not seem to view the word endings as structural or meaning elements in the words but rather as additional sounds which must be represented. *Asked* may be spelled ASKT, *scared* may be spelled SKARD, *teaches* may be spelled TECHEZ, and *watched* as WHACHT.

A clear example of a child in the phonetic stage of spelling development is seen below:

I LIKE TO ET SNO. DONT ET YELLOW SNO BEEKOZ IT IS WAR A DOG WAT. (I like to eat snow. Don't eat yellow snow because it is where a dog went.)

Tiffany uses phonetic strategies to spell words such as *like, eat, snow, because, is, where,* and *went.*

The *structural stage* occurs somewhere during the middle elementary years. During this stage, children begin to represent both short and long vowel sounds correctly, although the long vowel sound may still have the incorrect vowel marker. *Make* may be spelled MAIK or *gate* may be spelled GAET. The important distinction here, however, is that the child knows he or she must use a vowel marker (which is different than the child in the phonetic stage, who uses only the letter name of the vowel). Word endings are represented correctly in this stage, although there is still some confusion over when to double a consonant if an ending is added. *Getting* may be speled as GET-ING, *making* may be spelled as MAKKING, or *rider* may be spelled as RIDDER. This confusion appears to continue throughout the elementary years and reflects the child's lack of knowledge about the relationship between pronunciation and spelling (Beers and Beers, in press). Another common spelling error at the structural stage occurs with the schwa sound in words with unaccented syllables. Misspellings like BUTIN, BUTAN, or BUT-TUN for the word *button* are not uncommon at this stage, especially if the unaccented syllable is one other than the first syllable of a word.

The final spelling stage that presents difficulty for students can be called the *meaning/derivational spelling stage.* While many of the common spelling errors found in the writings of younger children have disappeared, other errors emerge as students attempt to deal with alternate forms of words or more sophisticated vocabulary with Greek or Latin roots. Reliance on the phonetic spelling of alternate forms of similar words seems to be central to these spelling errors. For example, a student may spell the words NASHUNAL (*national*), DAFINITION (*definition*), and CONCENSUS (*consensus*) even though the same student may spell correctly *nation, define, consent.* When students recognize that alternate forms of words are related by spelling and meaning even when their pronunciation changes, they begin to rely less on phonetic spelling for the alternate form of a word.

With the emergence of correctly spelled alternate forms of words and derivational forms of words, students have learned that pronunciation, structure, and meaning in words are all related to their spelling. A summary of these spelling stages is given in Table 1.

Table 1
Stages of Spelling Development

---

1. Prephonetic
   a) Letters used for words.
   b) No discernible letter/sound patterns.
   c) Letters may be continuous or separated.
   d) Generally unreadable.

2. Early Phonetic
   a) Phonetic word boundaries present.
   b) Single phonetically appropriate letter for word.
   c) Initial/final consonants appear.
   d) Certain letters regularly omitted, especially vowels.
   e) Somewhat readable.

3. Phonetic
   a) More consonants spelled correctly.
   b) Long vowel letters appear, often without markers.
   c) Short vowels appear as letter names.
   d) Later, these short vowels are spelled correctly.
   e) Endings often spelled phonetically.
   f) Readable.

4. Structural
   a) Short/long vowels spelled correctly.
   b) Endings spelled correctly.
   c) Doubling errors at syllable junctures with endings.
   d) Spelling errors with schwa-syllable spelling.

5. Meaning/Derivational
   a) Doubling errors with short/long vowel words less frequent.
   b) Common errors in words with alternate forms.
   c) Frequent errors in derivational forms (Latin, Greek, etc.).

6. Correct Spelling

An additional comment should be made about these stages. Children do progress through them at different rates.

What does all this mean for the teacher? How can we help children progress through these stages? First of all, the teacher must provide many opportunities for children to write. Frequent writing helps make correct spelling automatic. Writing is, after all, an opportunity for children to apply what they know about spelling in a meaningful context.

Secondly, a teacher of young children needs to give them time to learn about written words. When babies start to talk, the adults in their world do not expect them to talk correctly. They eagerly accept their renditions of "bottle" as BABA and respond positively to any attempts to communicate. In fact, we allow up to five years for children to master the oral language system. The same should also be true for children who are just beginning to write. We need to give them the gift of time as they begin to write, so that their attempts are treasured and responded to in the same positive manner. Teachers should make comments responding to the intended meaning of a written communication, not its spelling. Responding this way provides the child with the kind of warm and supportive response most likely to increase the child's writing attempts. What would happen if the teacher instead wrote the correct spelling of all misspelled words in red ink right above the child's words? Perhaps nothing initially. But over a period of time, the child who receives red ink marks is likely to do one of two things: stop writing altogether or write stories which contain only those words which are known. Either way, the effect is detrimental in terms of helping the child to see the importance of writing as a powerful communication tool. So allow each child to learn about written words and how they are represented. Do not insist on accuracy. Respond to the intended meaning rather than the structural elements of the writing at the beginning stages.

Another strategy which the teacher should use as children develop writing fluency is to ask them to spell the best they can when they come to words they don't know how to spell. That may mean asking the child "How do you think it is spelled?" or "How does it sound to you?" At this point, we want to encourage children to make use of the sound system as they spell. Our studies have shown they do just that very naturally. We want them to know that that is appropriate. Once students realize that their papers will not be red-marked for incorrect spellings, they are more willing to take the risk to spell a word they don't know by sounding it out. Fluency increases as a result.

Additionally, the teacher might find it helpful to recognize the fact that children's spelling development occurs at different rates. One child, for example, may benefit from spelling instruction that focuses on long *a* spelling patterns. Another may still need instruction on some simple letter-sound correspondence. To have both children working on the same page in the same book or with the same list of spelling words may not be helpful to either one.

Students will also find word exploration activities or word sorts helpful in learning about the various features that control the way words are spelled in English. Sorts can help students see that there is a great deal of regularity in English spelling if they know where to look for it. By examining words that have similar spelling patterns, children may more easily store and retrieve correctly spelled words. Such categorization of words and information about words can even facilitate long-term memory.

Word sorts should encourage students to examine the similarities and differences among known words. Words should be explored in terms of their pronunciation, structural elements, and meaning elements. Since we already know that children move from sound to structural to meaning elements in words as they go through school, these are the basic elements that should be explored from grade to grade. Primary grades should contain word-sorting activities that attend to the pronunciation of words, middle elementary grades should add sorts on structural elements in words, and the upper or middle school grades should include sorts on alternate forms and derivational forms of words. The general format for these word exploration activities or sorts includes the following:

1. Gather a collection of words that children know (through a word bank, writing material, actual reading material).
2. Ask the children to group the words according to some common feature that you provide or students try to identify. Some of the categories might include: short-vowel words, long-vowel words, one-syllable words, describing words, verbs ending in *ing*, past-tense verbs, words with prefixes or suffixes, similar forms of the same word.
3. Once a category has been filled by the students, ask the following questions and discuss the responses:
   Why did you put these words together?
   What do you find similar about these words?

What do you find different about these words?
Why is this a useful way to group words?

Through this process of examination and discussion, children reveal their notions about written words and discover aspects of words that they may be ignoring. Their responses also give teachers insight into their students' spelling strategies and what they know or do not know about words.

Here is an example of a word-sorting activity that was given to a group of third-graders. This particular group had difficulty correctly spelling words that ended in a / k / sound (*stick, strike, speak*). The teacher gave the group a list of words on the chalkboard (each word could have been on a single card so that each student had a card with each word). The words were: *strike, stick, break, broke, track, spoke, back, rock, rack, speak, bake,* and *speck*. These words were known to the students but were along with similar examples misspelled at the location of the / k / sound. First, the students came up with the following groups:

speck	strike	break
stick	broke	speak
track	spoke	
back	bake	
rack		
rock		

When asked why they had grouped the words this way, the students responded that the first group ended in *ck*, the second ended in *k* and silent *e*, and the last group ended in just *k*. Further discussion by the students led to the recognition that all the *ck* words had a short vowel before the / k / sound, and the rest of the words did not. One child asked, "Well, if I don't hear a short vowel before the / k / sound in a word does it always end in *ck*?" Another remarked, "Maybe only long-vowel words have only *k* and not *ck*." Further search through dictionaries for words that ended in *ck* or *k* or *ke* seemed to confirm for these students that matching the vowel sound to the / k / sound seemed to help in knowing when to end a word with *ck*. They concluded, therefore, that this was useful information to remember the next time they wanted to spell a word that ended in a / k / sound. Simple examination and exploration, helpful discussion in sorting out the information about the words, and no need to spell the words a hundred times. That is what word sorts can do for students learning to spell and learning about spelling.

What is particularly important to recall is that learning to spell is like any other aspect of language and literacy development. Children need opportunities to spell and misspell just as they did when they learned to talk and mistalk, write and miswrite. It is the primary way that humans learn, acquire knowledge, and use it effectively. Just like learning to talk or write, however, learning to spell requires interaction not just between children and their spelling attempts but also with correct spellings, and discussion about pronunciation, structure, and meaning and their relationship to spelling. "Spell it the way you think" and "Don't think about spelling" are helpful with young children as they begin to write, but guidance and input about spelling are also essential for spelling development.

References

Beers, Carol S., and James W. Beers. *Children's spelling of English morphology in the primary grades.* In S. Templeton and D. Baer (eds.), *Foundations of the word: Developmental orthographic knowledge of English.* Hillsdale, NJ: Lawrence Erlbaum Associates, Inc. (in press).

Henderson, Edmund E., and James W. Beers (eds.). *Developmental and cognitive aspects of learning to spell: A reflection of word knowledge.* Newark, DE: International Reading Association, 1980.

Read, Charles. *Children's categorization of speech sounds in English* (NCTE Research Report No. 17). Urbana, IL: National Council of Teachers of English, 1975.

Templeton, Shane, and Donald Baer (eds.). *Foundations of the word: Developmental orthographic knowledge of English.* Hillsdale, NJ: Lawrence Erlbaum Associates, Inc. (in press).

Developmental Aspects of Learning to Spell

J. Richard Gentry

A group of children ages four to seven invent spellings for "mon-ster" to label an illustration of *Where the Wild Things Are*. Jamie strings T-R-R-N-L together to form the word. Kim's spell-ing, MTR, correctly maps letters to three of the word's pho-nemes. MOSTR, Stacy's spelling, is a complete phonetic representation. A more advanced spelling by Dale, MONSTUR, visually stimulates correct spelling and follows conventions of English orthography. Each of the children have responded at a different developmental stage of spelling.

Learning to spell, a language learning process, like learning to speak, is developmental. Developmental stages of speech acquisition are familiar to most of us. The child begins the proc-ess at birth, a process driven by the individual's need to make sense of the world. From the outset the child receives language and responds in an attempt to make sense of the language in his environment. The child's oral language advances qualita-tively: babbling gives way to one-word utterances like "mama" and "cookie;" an inchoate syntax in expressions like "Daddy bye-bye" and "all gone milk" over time is replaced by mature speech reflecting substantial knowledge of pragmatic, semantic, syn-tactic, and morphological aspects of language (Menyuk 1977).

The developmental process continues to occur throughout the school-age years as children finely hone their knowledge of morphophonological rules and syntax (Menyuk 1984). These changes indicate that language develops not only as a simple increase in knowledge acquired, but also as a changing state of knowledge. The state of knowledge of the babbler is qualita-tively different from that of the baby who requests "cookie," and different still from that of the toddler who says "all gone milk." Similar qualitative changes tracked in children's early attempts to spell lead the educator to new insights on how spell-ing competency might best be accomplished.

Acquisition of written and oral language proceeds in much the same manner. Learning to spell, like learning to speak, is best viewed as a complex cognitive activity that advances with qualitative changes in the child's state of knowledge. These changes in the state of the child's orthographic knowledge are apparent in the written productions of normally developing children, and, if the preliminary evidence holds up, in most learning disabled children as well (Gerber & Hall, in press). This paper discusses the occurrence of developmental spelling and presents a theory base for teachers.

Review of Major Studies

Substantive research supports a sound theoretical base for the belief that learning to spell is developmental. The theory has two bases, one in the study of the nature of orthography and a second in the study of the nature of the learner. Theoretical foundations include the notion that English orthography may be consistent rather than inconsistent when viewed as a system that represents language. The consistency lies in levels beyond the widely recognized and often criticized lack of letter-sound correspondence in English (Chomsky & Halle 1968). Studies of the effect of orthographic structure and cross-cultural comparison of spelling systems in different languages provide additional research and theory base for describing the complexity and developmental nature of spelling (Read & Hodges 1982).

Research on the nature of the learner includes major studies of young children's intuitive application of their knowledge of English sound structure to spelling; speech sounds are categorized by four-to-seven year olds in ways that lead to systematic and logical, though inaccurate, invented spellings (Read 1971, 1975). Other researchers looking at school-age children have identified and described developmental stages of young children's spelling ability (Beers & Henderson 1977; Gentry 1978, 1982a; Templeton 1979; Zutell 1979). In total, these studies support a view that learning to spell is a multifaceted complex process and that cognitive aspects of learning to spell have implications for teaching. In addition, Gerber and Hall conducting developmental studies with learning disabled children report evidence that spelling abilities of learning disabled populations follow normal developmental patterns though at a delayed rate (Gerber & Hall, in press; Poplin 1983). Carpenter & Miller (1982) found that even intermediate LD children spelled and used error patterns like their younger nondisabled counterparts (Carpenter 1983).

What Is Developmental (Invented) Spelling?

Developmental spellings are spelling patterns resulting from different strategies that children use at various stages of cognitive development. These patterns or error types change as changes occur in the state of the child's knowledge of English orthography. Though some of the error types may seem unusual, they change systematically and predictably. The errors change qualitatively over time as experiences with print effect changes in the child's view of how English spelling works. Development progresses from simple to complex production, from concrete to abstract representation. Children first appear to discover that spellings may be invented by directly mapping letters to sound (phonetic spelling), but later they drop their direct letter-to-sound matching in favor of a strategy (transitional spelling) that appears to place more demands on their ability to remember visual patterns. As development progresses, strategies for correct spelling become multifarious and more complex. Visual memory may take precedence over spelling by sound for spelling unknown words (Frith & Frith 1980). As children learn more about words, it is apparent that root words, prefixes, suffixes, and other morphemic structure, as well as etymology, become important considerations (Gentry 1982a).

What Causes Developmental Changes to Occur?

Apparently young children need experiences with print that nurture development similar to experiences that nurture oral language acquisition. They need opportunities to observe and use print in the form of many varied unstructured opportunities to write and spell. Informal experiences with invented spellings may develop the initial cognitive structure on which eventual spelling competency is built. The process extends over time, encompassing development through free writing and later through formal spelling instruction accompanied by composition, revision, proofreading, and word study. Development occurs naturally through experience as normally achieving children think about how to spell words as they write and develop a spelling consciousness.

What Does Developmental Spelling Look Like?

Researchers have generally agreed that there are five developmental stages of spelling: precommunicative, semiphonetic, phonetic, transitional, and correct (Gentry 1982; different authors have labeled these stages differently, but with essentially the same intent). These spelling patterns occur naturally along with rote memorized spellings in young children's compositions. At five years of age, for example, Meredith wrote the following story about her cat using a preponderance of phonetic spelling:

WHER TOBE SLEPZ
HE SLEPZ IN THE NORNN ON A DAC
AT NIT HE SLEPZ N A GARJ

WHERE TOBY SLEEPS
HE SLEEPS IN THE MORNING ON A DECK
AT NIGHT HE SLEEPS IN A GARAGE

A sample of Meredith's composition at six illustrates advancement to the transitional level:

MY BABE STORE
I WAS BAORN IN JANUERRE
I WAYED AROUND 1 POUND
I WAR A WHIET DRES WITH
LASE ON IT.

MY BABY STORY
I WAS BORN IN JANUARY
I WEIGHED AROUND 1 POUND
I WORE A WHITE DRESS WITH
LACE ON IT.

If children are reluctant to write free compositions, developmental spelling may be elicited by having children spell words exhibiting particular sound features that induce different spelling solutions at different stages of development. Figure 1 illustrates developmental spellings of words at five different stages of development.

FIGURE 1
Five Developmental Stages

Precommunicative	Semiphonetic	Phonetic
BTRSS	MTR	MOSTR
OPSPO	E	EGL
APPO	TP	TIP
RTAT	A	ATE
BRSTA	UT	UNITID

Transitional	Correct
MONSTUR	MONSTER
EGUL	EAGLE
TIPE	TYPE
EIGHTEE	EIGHTY
YOUNIGHTED	UNITED

Guidelines for analyzing developmental spelling errors have been described in detail (Gentry 1982a, 1982b). An easy system for categorizing spelling errors is summarized below:

1. Precommunicative spelling. Spellers randomly string together letters of the alphabet without regard to letter-sound correspondence. Example: OPSPO = eagle; RTAT = eighty.

2. Semiphonetic spelling. Letters represent sounds but only some of the sounds are represented. Example: E = eagle; A = eighty.

3. Phonetic spelling. Words are spelled like they sound. The speller represents all of the phonemes in a word though spellings may be unconventional. Example: EGL = eagle; ATE = eighty.

4. Transitional spelling. A visual memory of spelling patterns is apparent. Spellings exhibit conventions of English orthography: vowels in every syllable, e-marker and vowel digraph patterns, correctly spelled inflectional endings, and frequent English letter sequences. Example: EGUL = eagle; EIGHTEE = eighty.

5. Correct spelling. The word is spelled correctly.

Specific Recommendations

New information regarding how spelling develops has led to better understanding of the kinds of activity that nurture spelling development. A list of instructional activities supported by developmental spelling research follows accompanied by a brief rationale:

1. Do not confine spelling to formal instruction. Although spelling is not learned incidentally, and children need formal spelling instruction (Graham & Miller 1979), spelling is a language-based activity, the development of which is dependent on many of the same intellectual and linguistic processes as reading, listening, and speaking. Spelling competency as a long-term goal is best achieved in an environment of whole language functional teaching, an environment that integrates the teaching of language arts and emphasizes functional use of language. Spelling complexity does warrant some isolated formal study, but spelling instruction should not be confined to formal study.

2. Induce children to write. Children need encouragement and opportunity to hypothesize about and create (invent) spellings. Invented spelling is naturally accomplished when children write to express their ideas or communicate their feelings. Children need opportunities to apply their growing orthographic knowledge in a variety of writing situations. These include any activity in which children write for the purpose of sharing information in print. Writing may occur at many levels. Appropriate forms for children include labeling, making signs, writing lists, writing plans, story writing, and writing songs, recipes, and letters. Every writing situation becomes a potential source for learning more about how the English spelling system works.

3. Encourage invented spellings and phonemic segmentation. This recommendation is particularly applicable to children at the early stages of learning to spell. When children are encouraged to spell a word as best they can or induced to invent a spelling, they engage their cognitive structures for spelling. They hyopthesize the phonemic segmentation of the word and select letter correspondences from the available logical alternatives. This is important activity for learning to spell. When children invent a spelling, they must think about how to segment the phonemes in a word. Phonemic segmentation not only forms a scaffold to which growing orthographic knowledge may

be added, it may also facilitate beginnings in reading (Ehri 1980).

4. Make allowances for inexperience with print. Children should write every day, yet all of their writing should not be held accountable for adult spelling. (Two year olds developing oral language competency are certainly not expected to speak like adults!) Allowances include judicial freedom from mechanics and de-emphasis of correctness in favor of more experience with spelling and greater levels of production. The teacher must place some trust in the belief that spelling quality will improve more rapidly if the child engages often in spelling production through writing. This is not a recommendation that spelling be learned incidentally. The revision process and requirements of correct spelling for "published" pieces are introduced early. Proofreading skills and consciousness of correct spelling are taught as part of the writing process. But the teacher's emphasis on expression and content over mechanics maintains central focus so that the child's interest and motivation for writing to communicate is held in esteem and remains intact.

5. Provide intense language experiences and word study. Daily language experiences should include opportunities to observe, verify, and correct spelling mistakes. Teacher conferencing and pupil self-analysis of spelling under teacher guidance are methods with proven results (Graham & Miller 1979). Highlighting predictability of spelling patterns through word sorting techniques is another highly profitable activity (Ganschow 1983; Sulzby 1980).

All that is good for spelling instruction is not new. While following the recommendations above, teachers should still keep in mind other tips with long-standing support from research:

— phonics instruction helps
— the list form works best with formal instruction
— children should correct their own tests under teacher direction
— the test-study-test method of formal instruction is superior to the study-test method (Graham & Miller 1979).

Learning to spell may not be simple, but more is being learned about how to teach it.

References

Beers, J.W. & Henderson, E.H. 1977. A study of developing orthographic concepts among first graders. *Research in the Teaching of English* 11: pp. 133-48.

Carpenter, D. 1983. Spelling error profiles of able and disabled readers. *Journal of Learning Disabilities* 16: pp. 102-04.

Carpenter, D. & Miller, L.J. 1982. The spelling of reading disabled LD students and able readers. *Learning Disability Quarterly* 5: pp. 65-70.

Chomsky, N. & Halle, M. 1968. *The sound pattern of English.* New York: Harper & Row.

Ehri, L. 1980. The development of orthographic images. In U. Frith (ed.), *Cognitive processes in spelling.* New York: Academic Press.

Frith, U. & Frith, C. 1980. Relationships between reading and spelling. In J.F. Kavanagh & R.L. Venezky (eds.), *Orthography, reading, and dyslexia.* Baltimore: University Park Press.

Ganschow, L. 1983. Teaching strategies for spelling success. *Academic Therapy* 19, 2: pp. 185-193.

Gerber, M., & Hall, R. in press. The development of spelling in learning disabled and normal students. (Monograph No. 1) Austin, TX: Society for Learning Disabilities and Remedial Education.

Gentry, J.R. 1978. Early spelling strategies. *Elementary School Journal* 79: pp. 88-92.

Gentry, J.R. 1982a. An analysis of developmental spelling in GNYS AT WRK. *The Reading Teacher* 36: pp. 196-200.

Gentry, J.R. 1982b. Developmental spelling: Assessment. *Diagnostic* 8: pp. 52-61.

Graham, S. & Miller, L. 1979. Spelling research and practice: A unified approach. *Focus on Exceptional Children* 12: pp. 1-16.

Menyuk, P. 1984. Language Development and Reading. In J. Flood (ed.), *Understanding reading comprehension.* Newark, Delaware: International Reading Association.

Menyuk, P. 1977. *Language and maturation.* Cambridge: MIT Press.

Poplin, M. 1983. Assessing developmental writing abilities. *Topics in Learning & Learning Disabilities* 3, 3: pp. 63-75.

Read, C. 1971. Preschool children's knowledge of English phonology. *Harvard Educational Review* 41: pp. 1-34.

Read, C. 1975. *Children's categorization of speech sounds in English*. National Council of Teachers of English Research Report No. 17. Urbana, Illinois: National Council of Teachers of English.

Read, C. & Hodges, R.E. 1982. Spelling. *Encyclopedia of educational research*. New York: Macmillan.

Sulzby, E. 1980. Word concept development activities. In E.H. Henderson & J.W. Beers (eds.), *Developmental and cognitive aspects of learning to spell*. Newark, Delaware: International Reading Association.

Templeton, S. 1979. Spelling first, sound later: The relationship between orthography and higher order phonological knowledge in older students. *Research in the Teaching of English* 13: pp. 255-64.

Zutell, J. 1979. Spelling strategies of primary school children and their relationships to Piaget's concept of decentration. *Research in the Teaching of English* 12: pp. 69-80.

A Developmental Perspective of Formal Spelling Instruction through Alphabet, Pattern, and Meaning

Edmund H. Henderson and Shane Templeton

For generations, pupils of varying ages have committed spelling errors like these:

WETR (winter)
JREK (drink)
ROBBIN (robin)
CONFUDENSE (confidence)
PORTIBLE (portable)
COMPATISHUN (competition)
DIFERENSE (difference).

Until recently, educators attributed spelling errors to such things as poor sound discrimination and inadequate visual and sequential memory. These interpretations are faulty, however, because they rest on two erroneous assumptions: (1) The spelling system of English is purely alphabetic and irregular, and (2) Pupils must learn most words by serial memory alone.

Research of the past 20 years in linguistics and in cognitive and developmental psychology explains far more adequately how students learn to spell (Henderson & Beers, 1980; Read & Hodges, 1982; Schlagal, 1982). This work demonstrates that English spelling can be taught systematically and that its mastery is not a peripheral skill but is central to literacy.

In this article we present information that supports this new perspective of spelling instruction. First, we examine the system of English spelling and note the different levels on which it represents information about the English language. Second, we present five stages of spelling knowledge through which achieving learners pass. For each stage, we outline the implications of developmental knowledge for direct instruction. We conclude with a discussion of the relationship between spelling competence and literacy.

Three "Ordering" Principles of English Spelling

There are three "ordering" principles in the spelling system of English: alphabetic, within-word pattern, and meaning (Henderson, 1984).

English spelling is *alphabetic* in that letters match sounds in a more or less orderly way from left to right. This is the level on which most speakers of English tend to think about the spelling system, and it is the variability of this letter-sound matching that is thought to be so daunting for young learners. A good example of this problem is the set of letter-sound correspondences represented by the consonant digraph *gh* in the words "ghost," "high," and "rough." Although Old English was spelled more consistently at the alphabetic level than English is today, the cumulative effects of foreign language borrowing, sound change, and the attempts to standardize spelling — largely a consequence of the printing press — have moved it further and further away from this primary level. The logic according to which letters are sequenced in Modern English becomes apparent only when the next two ordering principles are considered.

The *within-word pattern* principle illustrates why the consonant digraph *gh* can represent more than one sound. The occurrence of *gh* in words is not random: it depends on where the particular sound it represents occurs within a syllable. For example, *gh* can represent an / f / sound as in "rough" at the end of a word, but not at the beginning; at the beginning of a word it can only represent a / g / sound as in "ghost." The sound a letter or letters represent within a syllable depends on position and on the other letters that surround it. A more common example is the long vowel pattern signaled by a final *e* as in "fate"; children learn this pattern early, and it works well enough even though there are exceptions. The sound that *a* represents in this pattern depends on its environment, that is, the final single consonant and the final *e*. There are therefore patterns in English spelling, and although these letter units in particular sequences vary considerably, they are predictable. Furthermore, children can master these sequences when they know that such patterns exist and that it is pattern rather than simple alphabetic sequence that they must search out, attend to, and learn.

The third ordering principle in English spelling, *meaning*, is revealed by the fact that words or parts of words having the same or similar meaning tend to be spelled the same. For example, the spoken word /mēt/ when used to refer to a type of food is not spelled *meat* one time and *meet* or *mete* on other occasions. When it is used in this particular way — in reference to meat counters, meat eaters, raw meat, and so forth — it will always be spelled *meat*; the meaning fixes this particular spelling. When /mēt/ is used to refer to two or more individuals getting together, it will always be spelled *meet*; there is no question that the written phrase "going to a meating" is incorrect.

A sensitivity to the ways in which meaning is represented in the spelling system is required in order to note the common elements in more advanced vocabulary, such as the following word pairs: ins*a*ne-ins*a*nity, ser*e*ne-ser*e*nity, incl*i*ne-incl*i*nation, imp*o*se-imp*o*sition, impr*o*vise-impr*o*visation. In each of these word pairs, the italicized letters represent different sounds. Because the meaning in each pair does not change significantly, spelling maintains this relationship visually rather than changing to represent the changing sounds. This feature makes the spelling — and reading — of more abstract polysyllabic words in English easier. Awareness of this feature substantially enhances both spelling and vocabulary development.

Five Stages of Spelling Competence

The stages of spelling competence or knowledge predict the errors that pupils will make. Understanding and interpreting errors allow one to determine the particular word features that pupils need to study if they are to advance in spelling competence.

The basic unit of spelling is, of course, the word. Nonetheless, many children attempt to write before they understand this crucial concept. Accordingly, our account of how learners master English spelling must begin with this preliterate period, which is the first of five stages of word knowledge to be presented. These stages express the characteristics of children's strategies as they progress in their mastery of the spelling system.

Stage I

Preschool children who are read to and allowed to scribble freely will usually attempt to identify certain relationships between the marks they make and the sounds of language. Most of these attempts are tacit or subconscious; these children are not usually aware of the rationale underlying the relationships they establish. This urge to create written language extends beyond any particular socioeconomic class, culture, or language (Ferreiro & Teberosky, 1982; Harste, Burke, & Woodward, 1981). This process lays an important foundation for later word knowledge and for children's concept of what a word is, a concept that children develop only as they continue to attempt to read and write and are read to.

Consider the sample of a 4-year-old's spontaneous writing presented in Figure 1. Most children who create this kind of writing have learned three important things: They have learned about stories; they know what writing is (although they do not of course understand most of its conventions); and they know how to write letters and the names of the letters.

Fig. 1. — Sample of a 4-year-old's spontaneous writing.

Young children's "spelling" at stage I reflects their concept of the form and function of print, but it is not until stage II that they understand the first ordering principle of spelling, the alphabetic principle.

Stage II

Although children may not be able to describe their concept of what a word is — something like a sequence of letters between spaces — they will begin to spell alphabetically, matching sounds and letters systematically:

JRIG (drag)
LADR (letter)
MAK (make)
WETR (winter)
KEKT (kicked).

Although these letter-name spellings are alphabetic — matching letters to sounds in a left-to-right, sequential fashion — they are confusing to adults who know how English spelling actually works and who are not in the habit of thinking only in alphabetic terms (Beers & Henderson, 1977; Gentry, 1982; Read,

1975). These children are very close to the phonetic surface of their language. Often they note features of sounds to which adults no longer attend; spelling the beginning of "try" with *ch*, for example, is actually more correct phonetically than spelling it with *tr*.

As children proceed in this fashion, however, they are also beginning formal reading instruction with its related word analysis activities. From this experience, their store of sight words grows at a slow but systematic rate. Children tend to scan these words letter by letter, to recognize them automatically, and they usually spell them correctly. Sight words thus become the initial source from which children begin to learn the ways in which the spelling system represents speech. As children assimilate this knowledge and attempt to accommodate their own writing to it, they will advance beyond the simple linear or alphabetic transcription of speech to the more relational or pattern concept of spelling.

At this letter-name stage, pupils should begin to examine groups of words systematically. They are ready, in short, for a formal spelling program. Pupils must be able to read the words selected for study, and these words should be organized around a common, salient feature (e.g., short-vowel phonogram or beginning-consonant digraph). In addition, the features should require assimilation if students are to reach a higher level of development. For example, in order to identify the vowel nucleus and thus discover within-word spelling patterns, students must know that initial consonants and blends are separable units in a word or syllable.

Furthermore, children need to learn the Modern English alphabetic interpretation of short vowels. The word "pet" that they know at sight is spelled differently from what they would intuitively guess. Beginners think that the short *e* ought to be spelled *a*, that is, *pat*; similarly, they tend to omit the "nasalized" sounds that occur before consonants, as in "stamp" and "shrimp" (Beers & Henderson, 1977; Read, 1975). Analyses of children's spelling at stage II provide the following implications for instruction:

1. Ample time should be provided during language arts instruction for children to write creatively and purposefully. Students' attempts to spell words they do not know by sight or memory should be rewarded rather than condemned.

2. Teachers should provide instruction in letter formation and writing.

3. Students should be guided to examine and learn as correct spelling words a carefully drawn vocabulary from the words they are being taught to read. From this vocabulary the teacher should provide short lists of simple words to be memorized. These lists will reflect the principles in guidelines 4, 5, and 6.

4. Using their sight words and spelling words, children can practice recognizing, grouping, substituting, and spelling words according to the beginning-consonant element: single consonants, common-consonant digraphs (e.g., *ch, sh, th*), and common blends (e.g., *tr, dr*).

5. Teachers should present each short-vowel pattern systematically. Students should learn words containing these patterns both phonetically and by the pattern that governs that particular vowel.

6. Students should examine "continuant" or nasal sounds that occur before consonants (e.g., wi*n*ter, sta*m*p).

7. Students should also learn to spell a selection of the most common long-vowel patterns that occur in children's core vocabulary.

Stage III

As children attend to the features listed for stage II, their advancing word knowledge leads them to spell words in ways characterized by the following invented spellings:

HIEK (hike)
CREME (cream)
LETER (letter)
SPLINTIR (splinter)
PACKD (packed).

Children who are moving into stage III can give the correct or standard representation of short vowels, and include a silent vowel letter along with a sounded one in long-vowel words, as in the spelling of *raek* for "rake." They are moving beyond the surface of speech sound and beginning to form the within-word pattern principle. It is important to note that at this point children are able to read silently, and their oral reading becomes more natural.

This new perspective on words requires a degree of cognitive maturity, for there is a qualitative leap between the construction of words letter by letter from speech and doing so by sequenced units. The learner must attend simultaneously to sound and to pattern (Zutell, 1979). Thus it is not surprising that children advance to this competence through a period of awkward effort. At first they fumble about in a syllable, noting this at the end and that in the middle. Only gradually can they identify the pattern at a glimpse or write it automatically.

As children learn long-vowel spellings, they lay the foundation for an understanding of the open/closed syllable conventions of English; this understanding will serve them well in their later attempts to spell more complex polysyllabic words. There are two conventions governing long-vowel patterns in single syllables: the open syllable as in "me" (consonant/single vowel) and the closed pattern, in which a long vowel is indicated or marked by a silent vowel letter as in "cake" (vowel/consonant/silent marker) and "maid" (vowel/silent marker/consonant). There are, of course, several spelling patterns for each long vowel, but they are governed by principle. As children examine these patterns and represent them correctly in their writing, they learn — again, usually without conscious awareness — that some patterns are more frequent than others and that the patterns are conditioned by their environment. For example, syllable-final long *a* is rarely spelled *ai* but quite often *ay*; similarly, *ay* is hardly ever the spelling for a medial long *a* sound.

Students can examine, compare, and contrast several other vowel patterns at this stage. Most of these patterns are predictable, though some occur more often than others. The patterns include *r*-influenced vowels, as in "car" and "bird," and various vowel digraphs, such as *ou* in "could" and "should" and *au* in "pause."

It is tempting to provide children at this stage with rules; indeed, the examples above could quite nicely be phrased by rules, and children could be required to parrot them. The rule, however, is rarely what teaches the pattern and the features that control the spelling of the pattern. Rather, correct performance comes from experience in examining each pattern as it is met.

At stage III, children also begin to deal with the third ordering principle of spelling, meaning. Readiness for this new relational feature is first apparent when children begin to spell correctly the past tense ending -ed, despite its variation in sound (/ t / as in "clapped", / əd / as in "wanted," and / d / as in "saved"). This beginning awareness, coupled with students' foundation in vowel patterns, prepares them to learn the role of meaning in spelling. Despite the different pronunciations that ed represents, it usually means "something that has already happened."

The study of meaning begins in earnest when students examine compound words and homophones, words that sound the same but differ in spelling, such as "meet"/"meat," "pail"/"pale," and "tail"/"tale." Homophones are not negative instances of the irrationality of English spelling, though they have often mistakenly been treated so in the past. Instead, they exemplify the fundamental principle that words that have similar meanings are spelled similarly (e.g., sailboat, sailor, mainsail; not saleboat, salor, or mainsale). Children do acquire this understanding and are not disturbed by the apparent surface conflict between one sound and two patterns, provided teachers present this idea positively rather than complaining about the "illogic" of the spelling system.

After they have studied homophones and begun to appreciate the connection between meaning and spelling of homophones, pupils are able to learn the consistent spellings and meanings of many prefixes and suffixes. Then the teacher can introduce the concept of stress or accent in relation to spelling, as in remove and sailor. In each of these words, the unaccented syllable contains a schwa or neutral vowel (/ə/). Sound is no clue to the spelling of the schwa in these syllables, but if students understand that the syllables are affixes, then meaning fixes the stable spelling. Many pupils misspell these unaccented syllables precisely because they are still spelling according to sound rather than meaning.

Spelling instruction at stage III, which is appropriate for most students at grades 3 and 4, must emphasize study of the basic pattern features of words. Most important, students should know where to look at these ordering patterns within words they can read. The meaning principle also emerges at stage III. Instruction should include the following topics:

1. Review basic long-vowel patterns taught at stage II. Students

should examine additional common long-vowel patterns at this stage (e.g., /ā/; bait, weight; /ī/: light; /ē/: meat, freeze).

2. Common diphthongs are introduced (e.g., how, boil).

3. Students should study the r- and l- influenced vowel patterns (e.g., card, fern, fall, pull).

4. A beginning understanding of the power of the word-combining principles in the English language emerges from the examination of compound words. Students should study the subtle differences in relation between the two words that make up a compound. Sometimes the relationship is straightforward, as in "sailboat"; other times it is more abstract and often figurative, as in "heartbroken."

5. Students should learn the function of homophones in spelling.

6. Common inflections and the ways in which they are joined to base words should be examined (e.g., -ed, -ing, -ly). Understanding these conventions depends on an understanding of the common- and short-vowel patterns studied previously.

7. Teachers present the concept of base words, that is, that a base can stand alone after prefixes and suffixes are removed. More information on this concept can be presented after students have worked with inflections.

8. Students should study not only the sond but also the meaning of common prefixes and suffixes.

Stage IV

As students gain understanding of within-word patterns at stage III, their spellings will reflect the following errors:

    INOCENT (innocent)
    INVISABLE (invisible)
    FINANSHALY (financially)
    IMEDIATELY (immediately)
    DISSAPEAR (disappear)
    ROBBIN (robin).

These misspellings are due to an incomplete understanding of several conventions that guide spelling where syllables join together. Students' mastery of within-word patterns, primarily in single-syllable words, at stage III is necessary but insufficient for untutored spelling success with polysyllabic words. These conventions of "syllable juncture" begin at stage IV with an understanding of the rationale underlying the joining of common inflections to single-syllable words ("matting" vs. "mating"). Eventually they include the role of vowel pattern within a single-morpheme word ("rabbit" vs. "hotel") and the role of stress in a word with more than one morpheme ("referring" vs. "conquering").

In the cases of "matting"/"mating" and "rabbit"/"hotel," it is necessary that the various long- and short-vowel patterns be understood in order to learn whether or not a consonant is doubled at the point where the syllables join. In the first case, for example, "mat" contains a short vowel (the familiar CVC pattern) and requires the doubling of the final consonant; otherwise, the word would be "mating" — quite different in meaning, of course. In contrast, when -ing is added to "mate" the consonant is not doubled because, again, a different meaning entirely would result. These understandings are fairly well developed toward the end of stage III.

Consonant doubling occurs in "rabbit" because the vowel in the first syllable is short; it does not occur in "hotel" because the vowel in the first syllable is long. There are, of course, exceptions such as "robin" and "habit." For the time being, these are simply learned as exceptions, but, later on, students can study the historical and linguistic reasons underlying these seemingly exceptional spellings — there are, in other words, rules that often account for the exceptions as well.

In the case of "referring" and "conquering," whether or not the final single consonant is doubled before a suffix beginning with a vowel depends on whether the syllable is stressed: compare re*fer* (double the final consonant) and *con*quer (do not double the final consonant).

There is a common consonant-doubling phenomenon that relies more on meaning than on any other feature such as stress or vowel pattern. This phenomenon is termed "prefix assimilation" because the sound and spelling of prefixes are absorbed or assimilated into the base or root word. The phenomenon may perhaps best be explained through the following example. The word "immoveable" comprises a prefix originally spelled *in-* (meaning "not") plus the word "moveable." If "in" and "moveable" are blended together and pronounced rapidly, the sound represented by *n* approaches the pronunciation of the first sound, /m/, in "moveable." Historically, the same blending or absorbing of the prefix into the base word occurred. As these two sounds were assimilated into one, the spelling changed to reflect this assimilation. Other examples of this process include *ad-* (meaning "to" or "toward") + "prove": = "approve"; *ob-* ("toward" or "against") + "pose" = "oppose."

Once again, students' (in grades 4-6) knowledge of word structure determines what word features they should examine. A plan for such study should be based on the following guidelines, taking into account pupils' more advanced reading vocabulary:

1. Students should continue to study both common and uncommon vowel patterns in stressed syllables. Students need to be aware that the vowel patterns in the stressed syllables of two-syllable and polysyllabic words are usually spelled the same as the corresponding patterns in single-syllable words. For example, the vowel spelling in the CVC*e* pattern in "broke" is apparent in the stressed syllable of "revoke"; the vowel spelling in the CVC pattern in "flap" is the same as in the stressed syllable of "shatter".

2. Teachers should emphasize the characteristics of unstressed syllables, by teaching students to scan words systematically, syllable by syllable, noting the patterns. To do this, students will naturally pronounce a word, first noting as in guideline 1 above that the stressed syllable is usually spelled the same as single syllables and, second, noting how the unstressed syllable is spelled. Words with similar spelling of unstressed syllables may be grouped in order to discover why that particular pattern occurs.

3. Further examination of prefixes and suffixes with emphasis on the primacy of meaning over sound is necessary. Attention can be given to the conditions under which *-able* and *-ible*, for example, are used, as well as to *-ant/-ance* and *-ent/-ence* alternations.

4. Students should explore homophones, including those that are multisyllabic. This latter group comprises words such as "record" and "entrance," the pronunciation of which changes depending on the placement of stress.

5. The principle of consonant doubling is presented as it applies

to a broader range of vocabulary. Students now consider stress and syllable structure as well as vowel pattern in determining whether consonants are doubled at the juncture of suffixes or prefixes and base words.

Stage V

The principle that "words that are related in meaning are often spelled similarly" gains full force when students reach stage V (Templeton, 1983). The derivational relationships, or instances in which related words are derived from base or root words, that students began to explore at stage IV are now extensively developed.

One pattern that illustrates this principle is the silent/sounded consonant in related words. The silent *g* in "sign" and the silent *n* in "condemn" can be understood by noting the similarity in spelling between these words and words to which they are related in meaning, including "signal," "signature," and "condemnation." Despite variations in sound across these related words, the spelling visually preserves their meaning relationships.

Once students understand the silent/sounded consonant patterns, they can study the intricate but predictable system of *vowel alternations*. These entail most of the major derivational relationships in English spelling. Recent research suggests that students learn these alternations in a sequence (Templeton, 1979; Templeton & Scarborough-Franks, in press). Pupils begin with words in which an accented long vowel in a base word changes to a short vowel in the accented syllable of a derived word, as in div*i*ne-div*i*nity. Once students understand this pattern, they learn derivational relationships in which the long vowel in a base or root word alternates with a "reduced" vowel or schwa (/ ə /) in the derived word, as in def*i*ne-def*i*nition, comp*o*se-composition, and adm*i*re-adm*i*ration. Awareness of the principle underlying this second classification is extremely helpful: if students are uncertain about the spelling of the schwa in the second syllable of "composition," for example, they can think of the related or base word, "compose," in which the sound of the vowel is clearly heard and the spelling known.

Another pattern in which reduced vowels or schwas are apparent involves words in which a short vowel alternates with a schwa, as in loc*a*l-loc*a*lity and im*a*ge-im*a*gine. Students who are unsure about the spelling of the schwa in loc*a*l, for exam-

ple, can examine the spelling of the corresponding vowel in
loc*a*lity, in which the sound is clearly heard.

"Local" and "image" are but two of many words in which
the schwa causes consternation among students and teachers
alike. Because sound is no clue to the spelling of the schwa in
these two words, traditional wisdom holds that one must
memorize the spelling. This conclusion arises from a consideration of spelling on a word-by-word basis, exclusive of pattern
relationships. As soon as patterns are emphasized, however,
the logic and the primacy of meaning in the system become
apparent and are an obvious aid in both spelling and vocabulary expansion.

A fourth pattern of vowel alternation does entail changes in
spelling among related words, but such changes are regular and
predictable. For example, the sound and spelling alternations
in each of the following word pairs represent a pattern that may
be found in other words: ex*plain*-ex*plan*ation, re*ceive*-re*cep*tion,
pre*sume*-pre*sump*tion.

As pupils examine vowel alternation patterns, they should
also learn patterns of consonant alternations, knowledge of
which is a tremendous help to spellers. The first such pattern
to be studied is illustrated by the word pairs criti*c*-criti*c*ize,
attra*ct*-attra*ct*ion, and resi*d*e-resi*d*ual. In each of these word
pairs, the italicized consonant involves a change in pronunciation, although the spelling remains the same. Awareness of
this pattern dispels any ambiguity about representing the / s /,
/ sh /, and / dz / sounds, respectively, in each of the derived
words. A second consonant alternation pattern involves a
change in both sound and spelling, but once again this change
is predictable. For example, note the *t* to *c* alternation in
adolescen*t*-adolescen*c*e and complacen*t*-complacen*c*e (there is
no uncertainty about the spelling of the / s / in the second word
of each pair) and the *d* to *s* alternation in conclu*d*e-conclu*s*ion
and deci*d*e-deci*s*ion (no uncertainty about the spelling of / zh /
in "conclusion" and "decision").

Pupils' examination of the preceding patterns lays the ground-
work for a much more coherent and meaningful study of Greek
and Latin word forms as they occur in English spelling. Note,
for example, the function of *graph* ("writing") in bio*graph*y and
*graph*ology; of *tract* ("pull") in *tract*or, *tract*ion, con*tract*; and
of *spect* ("look") in in*spect*, circum*spect*, *spect*acle. Such forms
are often randomly presented in vocabulary programs for the

middle and secondary grades. As a result, many students retain very little related information. Alternatively, Henderson (1984) and Templeton (1983) offer systematic guidelines for this kind of study. It should be noted, however, that study of these elements establishes and reinforces an extremely important aspect of spelling: a "sense" or "feel" for the root or base as a meaningful element or unit, just as syllabic units, prefixes, and suffixes have come to be conceptualized as units.

There is no specific topic with which to end word study at stage V; students and teachers will always find fascinating details and hidden patterns. A formal spelling program at this level, however, should emphasize the following points:

1. Students should study several silent/sounded consonant patterns. In addition to the examples noted above, interesting pairs are resign-resignation, lim*b*-lim*b*er; a*m*nesia-*m*nemonic, autum*n*-autum*n*al.

2. Teachers should give considerable attention to the different vowel alternation patterns, sequenced for study as follows: (*a*) long-to-short (e.g., s*a*ne-s*a*nity, extreme-extremity, revise-revision; (*b*) long-to-schwa (e.g., infl*a*me-infl*a*mmation, comp*e*te-comp*e*tition, def*i*ne-def*i*nition); (*c*) short-to-schwa (e.g., exc*e*l-exc*e*llent, leg*a*l-leg*a*lity); and (*d*) predictable sound/spelling alternations (e.g., con*sume*-con*sump*tion, ex*plain*-ex*plan*ation, re*ceive*-re*cep*tion).

3. As students explore different vowel alternation patterns, they can also inspect various consonant alternation patterns that are quite predictable and often occur within words that have undergone vowel alternation. Examples of the most frequent patterns are listed with each of the two main categories of consonant alternation: (*a*) sound change/spelling stable (e.g., music-musician, constitu*t*e-constitu*t*ion) and (*b*) predictable sound/spelling alternation (e.g., explo*d*e-explo*s*ion, absen*t*-absen*c*e, permi*t*-permi*ss*ion).

4. The contribution of Greek and Latin forms to the spelling/meaning connection in English can be more profitably begun with the examination of Greek combining forms. Such forms as *graph*, *therm*, and *photo* usually retain a consistent spelling and meaning regardless of where they occur in words. As students gain an understanding of how these forms function, they can then move more confidently into the examination of Latin

roots, which, unlike Greek combining forms, are often hidden within words and occasionally undergo spelling changes across different words.

Study of Latin roots should begin with those that occur with great frequency and have fairly consistent spellings (Templeton, 1983). In addition to the roots mentioned above, a few examples are: -*pose*-, to put or place (ex*pose*, im*pose*); -*port*-, to carry (ex*port*, im*port*, *port*able); and -*dict*-, to say or speak (pre*dict*, *dict*ionary).

Conclusion

When English spelling is understood linguistically and its acquisition described developmentally, the process of learning to spell may be seen as a progressive cognitive mapping of a complex but orderly system. Knowledge of English spelling begins with the discovery of "word" and the application of the alphabetic principle of letter-sound representation. Learners progressively differentiate the alphabetic system into subsystems of pattern and meaning relationships. Through such order, English spelling achieves a near-optimal visual presentation of our complexly derived language.

Children learn to spell English directly by extrapolating new levels of order on the basis of words they know, use, and examine. Learning to spell is an active process, not a passive one. Furthermore, it is a concrete process, not an abstract one. Progress always entails word knowledge derived from reading and from applying the knowledge through purposeful writing. Spelling is thus pivotal to both reading and writing; in this sense it is central to the meaning and acquisition of literacy.

English spelling cannot be learned in a short time. Rather, its mastery parallels the acquisition of an adult vocabulary. What have made learning to spell English difficult have been our failure to understand clearly what children were doing as learners and our tendency to impose unrealistic standards for correctness. Even so, the traditions of English spelling instruction have for the most part been sound.

The critical event in spelling instruction is the requirement that pupils examine words. *How* students should examine words is a controversial issue. Some theorists and practitioners argue that spelling words should not be arranged into lists; they believe that such learning will occur through reading and writing. This conviction is in part a reaction to the ways in which lists have traditionally been organized and presented beyond the primary grades. The organization was often based on an inadequate analysis of the conventions according to which English is spelled. Now, however, our knowledge about the alphabetic, pattern, and meaning conventions of English spelling that deserve study, and the order in which they should be studied, suggests a more solid foundation according to which lists can be structured. In addition, students' progress in reading competence leads them further away from the detailed analysis of words that is necessary for spelling growth. To learn to spell words on the higher levels that the structure of English spelling reflects, students need to study words, to make discriminations, and to practice these routines of examining words; a spelling curriculum with the proper scope and sequence presented in a list format affords these opportunities.

Today most list words are selected, as they should be, by frequency counts of their occurrence in the language as a whole and in children's language in particular. Examination of basal spelling programs of the past decade for the primary grades will show a remarkable correspondence between the features derived from the stage theory presented above and the scope and sequence plans for word study. Greater divergence will be found, however, in some modern scope and sequence plans for the middle and upper grades. This reflects in part the fact that the study of Greek and Latin has largely been dropped from the curriculum. Until recently, formal spelling instruction did not evolve sufficiently to fill that gap.

Developmental theory validates the skills we should teach and provides a rationale for the pacing and maintenance of instruction in a more detailed and clearly stated manner than has been possible before. This achievement convinces us that English spelling can now be taught more effectively and not left to the blind forces of rote memory. What developmental research has achieved, therefore, is not a radical revision of traditional spelling instruction but a clarification of those things long practiced and, what is important, an extension of word study principles to the middle and upper grades, where they are presently most crucially needed.

There is of course another dimension to spelling instruction, the "informal" aspect — that which occurs in addition to the formal program. Because of its importance, this dimension is briefly addressed here. No author of a list-based series can know what a particular student's reading expertise is, the types of errors the student will make, or the student's dialect. Only the teacher has this information and can guide that particular student's spelling instruction on a day-to-day basis. Informal spelling instruction does more than teach a word or two; it conveys to students an attitude of inquiry and a routine for analyzing words.

Perhaps the most common situation in which informal spelling instruction occurs is in the reading group. Here, concerns about word analysis often reflect students' sensitivity to the context — the particular way in which a word has been used. In many instances, however, a word's structure is worthy of note, either because it may augment contextual analysis or simply because it is interesting in its own right. Particular consonant combinations, silent letters, vowel patterns, foreign words, special pronunciations — any or all may be relevant. In such cases, the teacher should encourage students to apply their spelling knowledge to the particular word; if similar words come to mind, fine; if not, the teacher can then supply a few. The teacher may guide an inquiry to determine whether the pattern under examination is common or rare and, if necessary, provide correct pronunciation. If discussion of meaning elements is appropriate, the teacher should guide the investigation, often leading the students to suggest other words that contain the same element; these discussions not only are enjoyable but also can help students to make connections among related words they already know.

The second situation in which it is often appropriate to teach spelling informally is in a writing critique or small-group conference session. Particularly with younger students — and after concerns with the intent and effect of the writing have been addressed — the teacher may ask, "Who will share a word that he or she attempted to spell but is not certain about?" This request conveys to students that the teacher expects and encourages them to attempt uncertain spellings when they write and that they should do so without fear of negative consequences.

A teacher who offers such spelling instruction knows the general sequence in which students master the different ordering principles of English spelling. Thus informed, the teacher is able to interpret students' errors, respond to their questions about words, and present examples of related words for examination. By planning for word study activities and responding to questions as they arise, teachers can better help students to improve their spelling.

This new perspective of spelling instruction as a central or pivotal element in the language arts curriculum may do much to pacify a long and bitter pedagogical dispute. With the emergence of formal reading methodologies in the 1870s, dissension arose between those who advocated learning to read by whole words with a primary emphasis on text, context, and understanding and those who advocated initial emphasis on letters, sounds, word parts, and word pronunciation. Before that time, reading, writing, and spelling were conjoined in what is now called the alphabet method. Today much methodological research appears to show a superiority for the second, or code emphasis, approach. At the same time, the dominant psycholinguistic view of language continues to challenge the compatibility of word study and reading fluency.

Perhaps these differences may be resolved by the recognition that children gradually master word knowledge and that this lengthy period of learning requires the study of words and the complex relationships among letters, letter patterns, and meaning units. Words to be studied can only be derived from *reading* and the exercise of word knowledge can occur best through *writing*.

Formal spelling study can include only a small sample of students' reading/writing vocabulary as it advances. Spelling texts present between 4,000 and 6,000 words. Literate persons read, write, and spell about 50,000 to 70,000 words. Students must apply what they learn in *formal* spelling instruction to reading and writing if they are to master the full vocabulary. Likewise, teachers should relate spelling instruction to the other two areas. *Informal* spelling instruction thus must occur during reading and writing. The key to this process is the word "apply." First and foremost, reading and writing themselves must be taught in the full richness of intellectual effort they require.

We believe that if teachers consider spelling instruction important and teach spelling with understanding and thoroughness, they can teach reading and writing with far greater ease and higher expectations for student learning. We believe that this is the true relationship of spelling to literacy for English speakers.

References

Beers, J., & Henderson, E. (1977). A study of developing ortho-graphic concepts among first and second grade children. *Research in the Teaching of English*, 11, 133-148.

Ferreiro, E., & Teberosky, A. (1982). *Literacy before schooling.* Exeter, NH: Heinemann.

Gentry, J.R. (1982). An analysis of developmental spelling in GYNS AT WRK. *Reading Teacher*, 36, 196-200.

Harste, J.C., Burke, C.L., & Woodward, V. (1981). *Children, their language, and world: Initial encounters with print* (NIE Final Report No. NIE-G-79-0132). Bloomington: Indiana University, Language Department.

Henderson, E. (1984). *Teaching children to spell English.* Boston: Houghton Mifflin.

Henderson, E., & Beers, J. (Eds.). (1980). *Developmental and cognitive aspects of learning to speak English: A reflection of word knowledge.* Newark, DE: International Reading Assocation.

Read, C. (1975). *Children's categorization of speech sounds in English.* Urbana, IL: National Council of Teachers of English.

Read, C., & Hodges, R. (1982). Spelling. In H. Mitzel (ed.), *Encyclopedia of educational research* (5th ed.) (pp. 1758-1767). New York: Macmillan.

Schlagal, R.C. (1982). *A qualitative analysis of word knowledge: A developmental study of spelling, grades one through six.* Unpublished doctoral dissertation, University of Virginia.

Templeton, S. (1979). Spelling first, sound later: The relationship between spelling and higher order phonological knowledge in older students. *Research in the Teaching of English*, 13, 255-264.

Templeton, S. (1983). The spelling/meaning connection and the development of word knowledge in older students. *Journal of Reading*, 27, 8-14.

Templeton, S., & Scarborough-Franks, L. (in press). The spelling's the thing: Knowledge of derivational morphology in orthography and phonology among older students. *Applied Psycholingistics.*

Zutell, J. (1979). Spelling strategies of primary school children and their relationship to Piaget's concept of decentration. *Research in the Teaching of English*, 13, 69-80.

PART III

Choosing a Spelling Program

At my son's school, spelling is taught from 9:45 to 10:45 each morning. I approach any criticism of the teacher with trepidation, since this school has been such a success in my son's two years there. I want to discuss with the teacher the merits of an integrated, holistic approach, but I hesitate, since the language program is giving my son such apparent strength.

The complex issue of deciding whether to integrate spelling into the program, or to handle spelling in the traditional method of direct instruction, is presented in this section. Judith Preen describes a whole-language approach to spelling, and Bob and Marlene McCracken present their popular spelling scheme for young children.

A Whole Language Approach to Spelling
Judith Preen

In *The Foundations of Literacy*, Don Holdaway (1979) writes:

> . . . we have seen that school instruction often fails when it moves away from developmental principles — when it moves from self-regulation towards teacher and programme domination, from intrinsic motivation toward extrinsic motivation, from self-pacing towards competition, from unified activity towards isolated skills, from authentic literature towards emasculated language and from deep meaning towards surface correctness.

Learning to spell is one facet of learning to write. A spelling program helps children become competent and confident writers. The British Columbia Language Arts curriculum guide (1978) states that good spelling is a result of a classroom climate in which a student has the desire, and feels the need, to communicate effectively. An obvious contradiction, however, lies in the fact that the prescribed spelling program focuses on structure and form rather than on meaning and purpose and does not suggest the developmental stages of spelling.

The following spelling approach explores successful developmental strategies and conditions for primary instruction, supported by current spelling research and underlying theories. The strategies and conditions are based on integration of spelling throughout the curriculum and focus on spelling as a process rather than a product.

This approach can be used with Grade 2/3/4 classrooms as an alternative approach to existing formal spelling programs in an attempt to free children to write and spell.

This spelling approach is based on current research relating to theories of spelling and language acquisition and the five developmental stages of learning. My program recognizes the findings of the writing-spelling connection and the importance of invented spelling in safe environments that encourage risk-taking. It also is in accordance with research supporting integration of spelling into the curriculum, and the reading-spelling connection.

Current research relating to language and spelling acquisition is based on the premise that children learn and grow naturally through developmental stages. This philosophy of using cognitive learning theory as it relates to spelling is supported by many researchers and writers. Booth (1985), Calkins (1986), Cochrane (1984), Forester (1980), Gentry (1987), Graves (1985), Holdaway (1979), Moffatt and Wagner (1983), Newman (1985), Templeton (1986), and Walshe (1981) verify that learning to spell is a developmental process that focuses on meaning and purpose rather than on structure and form. Learning how to spell depends on stages of spelling development, as does language acquisition (learning how to speak, read, and write). The researchers collectively agree that spelling is developmental and grows from understanding a system, not from list memorization.

A Spelling Approach

Based on the underlying theories and developmental stages of spelling, I wish to describe some general and specific strategies you may find valuable for practical application in the spelling components of the language arts curriculum.

General Spelling Strategies

DAILY WRITING

Calkins (1986), Cochrane and Cochrane (1984), Graves (1983) Holdaway (1979), Newman (1985), and Smith (1981) agree that writing is not a product but a process, that with the understanding of how children learn, teachers can provide a safe environment that provides the opportunity for pupils to write daily, to take risks, and actually learn to write and to spell.

Keep in mind a wide range of writing experiences for children. A common misconception is that children should be required to write in personal narratives only in writing classes. Consider the four dimensions of writing (function, mode, purpose, and form) to increase writing and thereby spelling development.

The dimensions are described here in summary, from Britton (1970).

FUNCTION

The three major functions are as follows:
Personal or expressive writing is loosely structured, free-flowing, and focussed on the writer.
Transactional or practical writing demonstrates an interaction with the world by writing in a practical way, and is focused on the information to be conveyed.
Artistic or poetic writing expresses ideas, and is focused on the language itself and its structure.

MODE

Researchers refer to common modes and genres of writing. The modes include narration, description, exposition, analysis, argument, persuasion, evaluation, and discourse.

The genres are fiction, poetry, personal narrative, familiar essay, argument, and exposition.

The terminology for writing models is not consistent; different authors use dissimilar terms for describing much the same thing. The important point is that you be aware of the dimensions of writing. It is your job as a facilitator of learning to provide examples of the modes and genres of writing and to encourage pupils to use them.

Purpose and form describe a wide range of possibilities available to the writer. The following list demonstrates how purpose and form are closely linked. It gives a useful framework for the writer to consider within the function of writing and the intended audience. Function, mode, purpose, and form are all interrelated; they depend on each other.

Purpose for writing	Writing form
To record feelings	Personal letters
	Poems
	Writing of sensory impressions from observations, stories, drama, music, art
To record observations	Data-recording
	Science reports
To describe	Character portraits
	Reports of a sequence of events
	Labels and captions
	Advertisements, e.g., want ads, lost and found
To inform or advise	Posters advertising coming events
	Scripts for news broadcasts
	Invitations
	Programs
	Menus
	Minutes of meetings
To persuade	Advertisements and commercials
	Letters to the editor
	Notes for a debate
	Cartoons
To clarify thinking	Note-taking for research topics
	Explanations of graphs, science diagrams, etc.
	Jottings
To explore and maintain relationships with others	Letters
	Greeting cards
	Making requests
	Questionnaires
To predict or hypothesize	Questions for research or interviews
	Alternative endings for stories
	Speculations about probable outcomes in health, science, and social studies topics

To compare	Descriptions
	Diagrams, graphs
	Note-making
	Charts
To command or direct	Recipes
	Instructions (how to make a _____)
	Stage directions
	Rules for games, safety, health, etc.
To amuse or entertain	Scripts for drama, puppet plays
	Stories and poems
	Personal anecdotes
	Jokes, riddles, puzzles
	Cartoons
	Pattern-writing

From Language Arts Committee (1979), *Writing: K-7 Language Arts*. Education Department of South Australia.

When allowing opportunity and variety for writing, you permit pupils to explore and to learn information about spelling patterns, sound/symbol relations, and grammatical and meaning relationships among words. Let children write freely without interruptions for standard spelling. It is a time for practising spelling as we are similarly allowed to practise speech.

During this writing time, the Cochranes (1984) stress, you must "take advantage of every opportunity to help students discover how words are spelled, to teach at the point of immediate need and to discuss meanings and the structure of words."

Invented Spelling

Have children write frequently. Allow children, during the first rough draft, to write freely without interruption or attention to standard spelling. Learning to spell is no longer considered to be mechanistic. Give children the opportunity to predict how they think a word should be spelled so they can check their predictions to see if they are correct. Give students the opportunity to make generalizations about words and their spellings. Since it is believed that much of the information about English spelling is not taught formally, children must abstract a system of rules and generalizations about the patterns underlying words. One of the strategies for allowing children to explore and to practise these patterns and rules is to invite invented spellings in the initial stages of their writing. Henderson (1981) suggests that children internalize information about the underlying rules and regularity that characterize the writing system, construct tentative rules, and then apply those rules in their writing.

Children are constantly changing their rule systems as they gain experience with language. Children develop a variety of strategies that also change in the way that their invented spellings and spelling errors change as they gain more control of written language and become more aware of spelling principles and spelling conventions.

Invented spellings and spelling errors offer valuable information about children's stages of spelling development. Using the information, you can help your pupils learn about spelling patterns, rules, and generalizations.

Much of the current research supports the idea that children need opportunities to formulate and test hypotheses about the writing system in a supportive environment where errors and invented spellings are considered a natural part of learning to spell.

You must encourage children to be risktakers. Conventional spelling should not inhibit the flow of writing in young children. Your correcting every spelling approximation with a red pen doesn't produce positive results. Children often conclude that the less they write, the fewer mistakes they will make. The opposite is true: the more children write, the fewer mistakes they will make — eventually.

Integration of Spelling with Reading, Writing, and Handwriting
Walshe (1981) states:

> Since spelling, by majority opinion, is more "caught" than "taught" the teacher's most important single spelling strategy will be an apparently indirect one: to provide an abundance of reading, writing and handwriting that is carried out in good spirit by the children. Within these activities, most of their learning of spelling will be going on unconsciously, subconsciously or consciously.

He further states that "reading means that the mind is registering impressions of standard spellings; reading is fundamentally a process of recognition which can aid in the visual memory of spellings." The implication for teachers is that they should provide ample opportunity for children to read during uninterrupted sustained silent reading, shared big-book readings, supportive readings, and readings of charts, lists, poems, etc.

Walshe (1981) says that "writing means bringing our impressions of spelling into conscious focus and pondering letters, syllables, probable letter sequences; spelling is fundamentally a process of 'recall' through 'writing.'" The implications for teaching strategies are outlined above under *Daily Writing*.

Handwriting means psycho-physical activity: *feeling* the letter sequences and meaning segments.

The more closely the total spelling program relates to class reading, writing, and handwriting, the more effective it will be.

You can derive more specific strategies from reading, writing, and handwriting sources. In reading, you can have children visualize and note the features of spelling words; in writing, you can have them predict their spelling errors by circling words they think they have misspelled, or you can have them list their errors; in both reading and writing, you can have children list common letter clusters, prefixes, and suffixes and practise them in their handwriting.

Specific Spelling Strategies

Hodges (1981) states:

> An effective environment in which to learn to spell is one that provides numerous and varied opportunities to master the patterns, generalizations, and anomalies of the writing system . . . spelling instruction cannot be restricted to the study of the relationship of letters to sounds, but demands an active involvement with both spoken and written language if students are to gain a functional understanding of the nature and uses of English spelling.

Hodges further asserts, "Spelling should be taught in the context of general language study . . . Learning to spell is a kind of holistic endeavour in which several aspects of word structure are experienced with each written language encounter."

With this focus clearly in mind, you can employ many spelling strategies within the context of the language-arts program.

SPELLING PREDICTIONS

Preschool and primary-school children use three language cueing systems to predict the spelling of words. Gentry (1977) and

Henderson and Beers (1980) define these cueing systems as follows:

Phonics. The knowledge of the names of the letters of the alphabet, coupled with knowledge of how sounds are articulated.

Grapho-phonics. The knowledge of the sound/symbol relationships.

Orthographics. The knowledge of the way letters are grouped into words. Within orthographics are three aspects to consider: sequence of letters, distribution, and orthographic patterns (e.g., made, fade, shade).

Children use these cueing systems to set up their own system of rules for spelling.

You must give children strategies that will enable them to attempt words they wish to spell. You mustn't provide lists of words: no evidence supports the notion that words taught from lists transfer to writing. Drawing the children's attention to the strategies that they already use in their predicting is one way you can encourage spelling development.

As pupils move toward the intermediate grades they add a fourth cueing system:

Morphology. The knowledge of patterns in word formation, affected by syntax (grammatical relations and functions of sentence structure) and semantics (the meaning within words, 'units of meaning' or morphemes, and the relationships of meaning between words).

All of these cueing systems operate simultaneously. All four may help to spell a single word, but often one strategy may be more useful than the other three for a particular word.

You can make children aware of these cueing systems through conferencing and small-group and whole-group lessons to enlighten them about their personal learning strategies and to take the mystery out of learning.

SOME SUGGESTED TEACHING STRATEGIES

The following teaching strategies can enhance your spelling approach. The strategies facilitate spelling development and provide alternatives to traditional spelling lessons.

Letter pattern observations. Draw attention to letter patterns or sequences that recur. McCracken and McCracken (1985) have listed in detail many of the recurring patterns children should recognize.

Examples are *ch, ck, ic, qu, ph, ing, ough, ong*.

Meaning units (morphemes, minimal units of meaning). Draw attention to obvious morphemes such as frequently recurring roots, prefixes, and suffixes.

For example, it is helpful for children to know that 'un' means 'not'.

Related spellings. When children are unsure of a spelling, draw attention to a word that contains the same root word, e.g., *nation* and *national*.

Clear articulation. Encourage using standard pronunciations. *"Have a go!"* Incite children to try writing words they cannot spell, to discover how the word feels and what it looks like. Have them circle words they are unsure are correct.

A spelling buddy. When children are 'having a go' during writing, and circling any words they are unsure of, have them ask a trusted buddy to read their work, underline any misspellings hc/shc finds, and be allowed to correct the circled spellings on top of the circled words.

A spelling log. Have pupils create individual or class word collections compiled in a dictionary format.

Proofreading. Give pupils copies of letters or short excerpts that contain spelling errors. Have the children examine the words in the material and underline any incorrect spelling. Explain that this procedure of reading written material and correcting the spelling errors is called proofreading. You can have pupils write the correct spellings above the underlined words and keep the proofreading sheets in proofreading folders.

Collection of poems. You can make the following poem or others into charts for children to read, to chant, and to conceptualize through your using a variety of teaching techniques. Collect poems that focus on English words, their regularities and irregularities.

Why English Is So Hard

We'll begin with box, the plural is boxes.
But the plural of ox should be oxen, not oxes.
One fowl is a goose, but two are called geese,
Yet the plural of mouse is never meese.

You may find a lone mouse, or a whole nest of mice,
But the plural of house is houses, not hice.
If the plural of man is always men,
Why shouldn't the plural of pan be called pen?
The cow in the plural may be called cows or kine,
But a bow, if repeated, is never called bine;
And the plural of vow is vows, not vine.

If I speak of a foot and you show me two feet,
And I give you a boot, would a pair be called beet?
If one is a tooth and a whole set are teeth,
Why shouldn't the plural of booth be called beeth?
If the singular's this, and the plural these,
Should the plural of kiss ever be written kese?
We speak of a brother, and also of brethren,
But though we say mother, we never say mothren.
Then the masculine pronouns are he, his, and him,
But imagine the feminine, she, shis, and shim!
So English, I think you all will agree,
Is the funniest language you ever did see.

Author Unknown

Graphic words. Using a card-filing system, have pupils print a word per card, using stylized printing, and decorate the word to express its meaning.

Examples:

Visualizing phrases. Print phrases so that the words communicate the meaning of the phrase.

Shaping. Outline a shape — a shoe, for example. Have children write relevant words along the line of the shape, or you can have them fill in the open spaces within the shape.

Example:

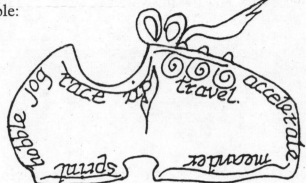

Alliteration fun. Senisitize children to alliteration in poems and stories. Collect tongue twisters, and have a tongue-twister challenge. Gather alliteration samples from newspapers and magazines. Create posters or collages. Create silly sentences using alliteration.

Wordles. Have children think of words or phrases in unusual ways. Use a bulletin board, a poster, or a small scrapbook to display the work. Examples:

SIDESIDE
(Side by side)

YOU/JUST/ME
(Just between you and me)

Once
Time
(Once upon a time)

STAND
I
(I understand)

Word demons. Provide a chart or a sheet with the following 100 words that are often spelled incorrectly. Use the word list for creating new games, crossword puzzles, word scrambles, and word searches.

ache	done	making	they
again	don't	many	though
always	early	meant	through
among	easy	minute	tired
answer	enough	much	tonight
any	every	none	too
been	February	often	trouble
beginning	forty	once	truly
believe	friend	piece	Tuesday
blue	grammar	raise	two
break	guess	read	used
built	half	ready	very
business	having	said	wear
busy	hear	says	Wednesday
buy	heard	seems	week
can't	here	separate	where
choose	hoarse	shoes	whether
color	hour	since	which
coming	instead	some	whole
cough	just	straight	women
could	knew	sugar	won't
country	know	sure	would
dear	laid	tear	write
doctor	loose	their	writing
does	lose	there	wrote

Dictionary skills. Introduce a dictionary, showing that it provides information on spelling, usage, antonyms, synonyms, syllabification, and meanings. Address specific skills for using the dictionary: alphabetizing and the use of guide words.

Instill in children the awareness that the dictionary is the most valuable tool a speller has.

Here are activities that children can engage in for practice and enjoyment.

1. Alphabetizing does have an important place in the study of spelling. Children need a knowledge of alphabetical order to

locate words in the dictionary. This knowledge also is an indication of pupils' awareness regarding letter sequences. Have pupils organize themselves in alphabetical order by the beginning letters of their first names or their last names.

2. When brainstorming within a category such as food, toys, sports, animals, or ice-cream flavors, have children alphabetize the brainstormed words. You can have children do this activity in small groups or individually, using flashcards or listing the words on charts.

3. See if the children wish to make a classroom telephone directory or, as a class project, attempt a school telephone directory.

Dictation. You or a student dictate spelling words, either from a word family or from another spelling source. Have the children, using small chalkboards, record their responses (predictions) on the board. You or the student leader can model the correct spelling on the large blackboard. Have pupils correct their own spellings. Have them circle the part that is incorrect and record the standard spelling on their chalkboards.

Transcribing. Writing down live or recorded messages gives pupils excellent practice in all of the encoding skills: spelling, handwriting, and punctuation. You may create many varieties of this activity.

Spelling lists. Create spelling lists that develop out of the current interests of the children, containing words that the children are using.

Mnemonic devices. If pupils have continued difficulty with a particular word, demonstrate to them or let them invent a mnemonic device to help them remember how to spell the word: You'll be my *friend* to the *end*.

Modelling curiosity. Wonder aloud about specific spellings, and show children how to discover the origins that account for the unusual spellings by using the dictionary.

Lists of words. Create or have children create lists of words from children's own interests and immediate needs.

Effective word-study techniques. Gentry (1987) suggests teachers "should provide guidelines for effective word study techniques . . . these would include visual inspection, auditory inspection, kinesthetic reinforcement, and recall — always with the words treated as wholes." Gentry provides two models he considers to be effective.

Fitzgerald method (1951)
Look at the word carefully.
Say the word.
With eyes closed, visualize the word.
Cover the word, and then write it.
Check the spelling.
If the word is misspelled, repeat the steps.

Horn method (1954)
Pronounce each word carefully.
Look carefully at each part.
Say the letters in sequence.
Attempt to recall how the word looks; then spell it.
Check your attempt to recall.
Write the word.
Check this spelling attempt.
Repeat the above steps if necessary.

Spelling Strategies Based on Developmental Trends

PREPHONETIC SPELLERS

Read aloud and often. Create big books.
Put words on walls and bulletin boards that label objects or pictures.
Have students develop picture dictionaries.
Use dictations and experience charts frequently so voice pointing develops.
Have students echo and choral read familiar stories and dictations.
Create sentence labels for displays and objects in the room.
Use pattern dictations or writing to focus on a word.
Develop word banks, and have students categorize words by common spelling elements.

PHONETIC SPELLERS

Using familiar words, have students develop word families for basic vowel-sound spellings.
Draw attention to CVC spelling patterns and sounds heard in words with such patterns.
Have students practise identifying the number of sounds in words they know.

Use a cloze technique with familiar words, and have students match the sound with the letter omitted.

Encourage students to write extensively using their best phonetic spelling.

Continue word-bank activities.

Have students perform word hunts with magazines, newspapers, and books.

Have students identify words with one syllable and with two syllables.

TRANSITIONAL SPELLERS

Using word sorts, review common consonant and vowel patterns.

Have students sort familiar past-tense words by the sound of the ending.

Focus on the connection between vowel spelling and spelling changes when *ing* or *ed* is added.

Do word sorts with long and short vowel words with *ing* or *ed* endings.

Have students do simple word expansion: happy, unhappy, happier, happily, happiest.

Continue word hunts.

Encourage writing.

Have students develop a personal dictionary.

Have children identify their own troublesome words.

Have them serve as spelling editors for each other.

Have students look for spelling patterns in two-, three-, and four-syllable words.

STANDARD SPELLERS OR MEANING/DERIVATIONAL STAGE

Review basic knowledge at transitional level.

Create word sorts that connect sound and spelling changes in words.

Conduct meaning maps. Start with words that have derivations.

Explore common Latin and Greek derivational forms.

Have students combine forms to make nouns or adjectives. E.g., microscope — microscopic, photography — photographic.

Have students use the dictionary to determine the origin of a word, its spelling and pronunciation.

Continue writing.

Traditional spelling programs do not acknowledge current

research. Whole language enthusiasts keep asking ". . . and what about spelliing?" The current research has provided a solid rationale for change. Educators need to be informed about language-acquisition theory, developmental stages of spelling, and the writing-reading-spelling connections in order to develop integrated, child-centred, and non-competitive spelling programs in a safe, risk-taking environment. The plaintive "I can't spell" must be replaced by joyful love words.

References

Booth, J., D. Booth, W. Pauli, and J. Phenix (1985). *East of the sun: Teacher resource book: Impressions.* Toronto: Holt, Rinehard and Winston.

Brittoro, J. (1970). *Language and learning.* New York: Penguin.

Calkins, Lucy M. (1986). *The art of teaching writing.* Portsmouth, NH: Heinemann Educational Books.

Cochrane, Orin, Donna Cochrane, Sharon Scalena, and Ethel Buchanan (1984). *Reading, writing, and caring.* Winnipeg: Whole Language Consultants Ltd.

Forester, Anne D. (1980). "Learning to spell by spelling." *Theory into Practice,* 19(3).

Gentry, Richard R. (1987). *Spel . . . is a four letter word.* Richmond Hill, Ontario: Scholastic-TAB Publications Ltd.

Graves, Donald H. (1983). *Writing: Teachers and children at work.* Portsmouth, NH: Heinemann Educational Books.

Graves, Donald, and Virginia Stuart (1985). *Write from the start: Tapping your child's natural ability.* New York: New American Library.

Henderson, Edmund H. (1981). *Learning to read and spell: the child's knowledge of words.* DeKalb, IL: Northern Illinois University Press.

Henderson, E.H., and J.W. Beers (1980). *Developmental and cognitive aspects of learning to spell.* Newark, Del: I.R.A.

Hodges, Richard E. (1981). *Learning to spell.* Urbana, Illinois: ERIC Clearinghouse on Reading and Communication Skills and the National Council of Teachers of English.

Holdaway, Don (1979). *The foundations of literacy.* Sydney, N.S.W.: Ashton Scholastic.

Language Arts Committee (1979). *Writing: R-7 language arts.* Education Department of South Australia.

Lehr, F. (1986). "Invented spelling and language development." *Reading teacher,* 39(5), 452-54.

McCracken, Marlene T., and Robert A. McCracken. *Spelling through phonics.* Winnipeg: Peguis Publishers.

Ministry of Education (1978). *Elementary language arts curriculum guide.* Victoria, B.C.

Moffatt, J., and B. Wagner (1983). *Student-centered language arts and reading, K-13: A handbook for teachers.* Boston: Houghton Mifflin Company.

Newman, Judith M. (1985). *Whole language theory in use.* Portsmouth, NH: Heinemann Educational Books.

Smith, Frank (1983). *Essays into literacy.* Portsmouth, NH: Heinemann Educational Books.

Templeton, Shane (1986). "Synthesis of research on the learning and teaching of spelling." *Educational Leadership,* 43(6).

Walshe, R.D. (1981). *Every child can write.* Rosebery, N.S.W.: Bridge Printery Pty. Ltd.

Teach Children to Spell

Robert A. and Marlene J. McCracken

There are three beliefs we would like to start with:

1. Spelling is a skill, and like all skills is acquired through meaningful practice.
2. As with any skill, spelling can be learned only to the degree it is understood.
3. Spelling is a language skill; as such it is learned through immersion, which allows the brain to intuit how spelling works.

Having stated those three beliefs, let us state what spelling is not. It is not the rote memorization of correct letter sequences, nor is "good spelling" the result of learning to spell words. Good spelling is not caused by good visual memory or auditory acuity and poor spelling by their lack. Good spelling is not the result of spelling lessons involving ten or more words per week.

Now, let's examine the three beliefs. We will not try to prove number one, other than to say that it is a fairly well verified belief, accepted as far as we know without serious challenge. We are aware of the danger of this argument because we challenge equally well verified beliefs in stating numbers two and three.

The spelling of words is systematic and rational if viewed historically. Men did not set out to make English spelling chaotic. They set out systematically to spell English speech with its more than forty sounds. Unfortunately they used the twenty-six-letter Roman alphabet to do this so that a completely regular alphabetic writing system was impossible. Subsequent changes in how words were pronounced caused the relationship between letters and speech to become even more obscure. Our chaotic spelling can be explained, but not to a child trying to solve the mysteries of print and spelling. This seeming chaos often prevents a child from learning how letters and print work, and until a child learns how letters work he or she can never become proficient in spelling.

Belief three says that the learning of spelling is intuitive; the logical corollary of this is that spelling cannot be taught. There is another possible corollary; spelling must be taught in such a way that intuition can function. We accept this latter notion and have developed a systematic scheme which we have detailed in *Spelling through Phonics* (Winnipeg: Peguis Publishers, Ltd., 1982). In our scheme spelling is learned through practising phonics while writing. Phonics is the major skill used in learning to spell. Our concern is to get children to understand that English writing is an alphabetic system. We want to teach children efficiently how to create a writing system so that they may understand how English print works.

Perhaps this is the place to talk about inventive spelling. Children always engage in inventive spelling once they learn that print is a form of language and that an alphabet exists. Some children come to school knowing this. Their parents have read to them thousands of times and filled them with language in many ways. The teaching was so natural and informal that these children seem to emerge into reading and writing and spelling without teaching. Many other children come to school with no knowledge of print. They must be immersed in a whirlpool of meanings and taught if they are to learn language. Language skills emerge only after children have been immersed in language and taught (informally or formally) how to play with language to learn how it works. To teach we read orally from books, and we track print. We sing and we chant. We manipulate print in a pocket chart. We take dictation on the chalkboard, and *we teach children how to spell and how to write*. We teach so that the children can invent spelling as a natural way in learning how to spell. We must teach efficiently. We dare not wait for children to emerge by themselves as spellers in grades three or four: we begin teaching spelling in grade one.

When children invent spellings, they are spelling as well as they can; they have not yet learned enough about how letters and print work to spell correctly. They need to be taught more so that they are able to spell better, and eventually correctly.

In *Reading Is Only the Tiger's Tail* (Winnipeg: Peguis Publishers Ltd., 1972, 1987), *Reading, Writing, and Language* (Winnipeg: Peguis Publishers, Ltd., 1979), and *Stories, Songs and Poetry to Teach Reading and Writing: Literacy through Language* (Chicago: American Library Association, 1986), we have described what would currently be called whole language teaching. Within such a program we teach spelling for five minutes a day to small groups of children. We demand that they practise as well as they are able while writing independently each day. We will summarize the spelling procedures here, and refer the reader to the above books and to *Spelling through Phonics* for a more complete explication.

Requisites for Learning How to Spell

Spelling requires two insights. First, children must intuit what a word is. Second, they must understand two concepts about alphabetic writing: a) spoken sounds are represented by letters, and b) the letters are written in the sequence in which the sounds are uttered. Children must realize that when you say a sound you write a letter, and that you write the letters in a left to right sequence.

We do lots of work with the pocket chart, using word cards and pictures to represent poems, songs, and nursery rhymes to develop a sense of what a printed word is. We do lots of chart and chalkboard work to develop beginning writing through frame sentences. This again develops a sense of the printed word. We teach the phonics of spelling in small groups, and we demand lots of writing and correct spelling in so far as it has been learned.

We begin formal spelling by teaching four things together. We teach the letter *m*, for example, by teaching:

1. the name of the letter;
2. the sound the letter represents;
3. the "feel" of the letter in the mouth;
4. the way the letter is written.

We do this with small chalkboards or by sitting around a chalkboard table. We tell the children that they will learn about a letter. We have the children say the letter name, and make the letter sound. We have the children feel what they do with their mouths in making the sound. For example, to reach / m /, we have the children say the letter name, *em*, asking them what they are doing with their mouths. This encourages them to associate the sound with the feeling. We show the children how to write the letter, and they print the letter on their chalkboards. We start teaching with consonants because vowels are so erratic in their representations, and because vowels cannot be felt and discriminated within the mouth.

All children have a penmanship book in which they practise making both capital and lower-case forms of letters. They write two lines of lower-case letters and two of capitals. They copy two to five words that they find around the room which contain the letter of the day. They each draw twenty to forty small pictures representing words that they know orally in which there is an *m* or the letter of the day. Most of the pictures will illustrate words that begin with / m /.

We teach six consonants before we teach any vowels, and then we introduce short / a /, followed by another six consonants. The abler children frequently generalize by this time and write quite freely, spelling phonetically, sequentially, indicating that they have grasped the basic notion of letters representing sounds in a left to right print sequence. Others will be struggling, only beginning to understand the notion after they have had several error-loaded lessons because they need to be taught ten or fifteen letters before they can generalize. We do not dawdle if some children seem to be having trouble. We will go back and reteach but we need to get enough taught so the children have a chance to understand how print works.

As soon as a vowel has been introduced we help the children spell whole words or syllables. In one sense, there is no such thing as an easy word or a hard word. All words are either single syllables or combinations of syllables. Most syllables are combinations of two or three sounds. There are words that are hard to spell in that they have unusual patterns or unexpected letter combinations to spell syllables. Thus *beaux* is harder than *bow*, which in turn is harder than the proper name *Bo* or the last syllable in *hobo*. If we have taught the letters *m, s, f, b, t, a* and the sequence *ing* and the child has learned them, we expect the correct spelling of *mat, stab, fast, Sam, bat*, and *bats*, but we also expect *fascinating* to be spelled *fasnating*, although the first *n* may be expecting too much since it has not been taught specifically. Most children who have learned those six letters and *ing* will generalize enough to use the *n* from *ing*.

The sequence of subsequent teaching varies depending upon the spellings that the children are using in their writing. We may teach:

1. another short vowel, usually / o /;
2. *s* as a plural whether pronounced / s / or / z /;
3. another six consonants [a total of eighteen have now been

taught];

4. the remainder of the consonants;
5. *y* as representing long / e / on the end of words so that children can spell words such as *sandy, badly, candy, rusty, lumpy,* etc.;
6. *ing* as an ending because children need *ing* to write freely.

In doing dictations we have begun the final step in teaching spelling, the teaching of patterns. Learning to spell becomes a lifelong process. For example, this paper is being written with both American and Canadian readers in mind. How should we spell *favor* (favour), *practice* (practice and practise), *check* (cheque as a bank draft)? Spelling is not an absolute. *Travelled* and *traveled, develope* and *develop,* etc. are all acceptable by some authority.

Some frequently used words are non-phonetic in transcription. If children are to write daily and spell these words as they anticipate they should, they will misspell these words so often that they will commit misspellings to memory. We call these words "doozers"; we post five of these prominently within the room and insist that children spell them correctly. We begin doozers in December in grade one and in September in all other grades. *They* is our most common doozer because some children spell *they* as *thay* and maintain this wrong spelling seemingly forever. *Does, because, is, the, come,* and *have* are doozers. Once a doozer seems to have been learned we replace it with another.

After December in grade one and after day one in all other grades we refuse to spell for pupils who ask how to spell. The children must spell as well as they are able in order to practise the phonics which they are being taught. The teaching is useless without the practice, the application. It is through practice that children internalize all of the *rules* they need for independent word recognition. The rules are intuited rather than directly stated. Intuited rules rarely are applied incorrectly; rules taught to children frequently are applied with poor results.

We teach children to spell syllabically and demand that they practise as they write. Their writing tells what they have mastered, what they are learning, and what they apparently need to be taught in their small dictation groups. We correct what we have taught by nagging children as they write. When a child has attempted a word beyond his or her ability, we nag to get spelling as correct as possible, so that just any spelling is not accepted, even though what we accept is not correct. Spelling becomes a phonics teaching program with daily writing the natural way to practise phonics.

We will not attempt to describe our daily writing program except to say that children from grade one on should engage in a variety of writing activities every day. Without lots of practise they are unlikely to become literate.

We teach no rules. Children come to understand three or four generalizations which enable them to make sense out of words and to understand how print works. This enables them to learn the horrendous patterns of correct English spelling, and to learn many peculiar spellings by merely encountering them in reading.

They learn that usually:

1. When you say a sound you write a letter. (They also learn that you sometimes write several extra letters to make one sound.)
2. Every syllable has a vowel letter in it.
3. Long vowels are often spelled erratically, and the short ones are not too dependable, either.
4. If it is really important, and you are not sure, the only way to spell a word correctly is to look it up.

We have had hundreds of reports from experienced teachers who have used the methods outlined here. They have reported four things over and over again. We will paraphrase as if quoting:

1. "My grade one children spell anything they need without fear. They love writing and want to write all day. They spell better than any class I ever taught before."
2. "My special ed children can write and I can read their work. I've never had kids who could write before; they could only copy and then they didn't know what it said."
3. "The children love their five-minute spelling lessons and want them to be longer and harder."
4. "I don't have to teach word recognition skills. The children just seem to know the unknown words when they read."

We want to show four typical examples of the writing and spelling of children exposed to our teaching methods. These are representative of hundreds of others that might have been chosen.

"My Kitten" is free writing in February by a grade one student who would rank at almost the middle of the class in overall performance.

> MY KITTIN
>
> Once upon a time there live
> a kittin (Wich was my kittin.)
> His name was tabutha. I
> heared him at my door. So
> I tooled my Mom. She bring
> him in. he was cold, and hungry.
> We gave him some mete, and we
> gave him some milk. Then the
> nxst day he has sik. The hole
> family looked after him. Now hes
> like a monster. In the morning,
> When I'm trining to get
> redy for school. He hides around
> kornrs. and then he pounsis
> on me. and now you know about
> my kittin.

Robert was in an all-Chicano ESL grade one classroom. His work in October was clearly the "worst" in the class. By December, as the second sample shows, he had improved a lot.

E1.

Once uypohnaalTime thin was a liTTe elve Crik in my Room when I Opn my iss I so Two elve Looking at me and Thi Look at me Thi Run a way The end

Robert Dec 16th

From the early 1980s, the following are samples from a grade two child who had immigrated to Canada from India and had entered school in the middle of grade one. The difference between September and January speaks for itself.

9-9-83

Las night I walk Home when I Home I Hq To lay down

Were you tired?

NO

1-26-84

Dear teacher
Yesterday what I don't no what happened would you tell me I don't no a singel thing about yesterday was anybody away expect me and David was there and would mind telling me about this play I don't no anything like filling me in about the play tell about it I'm blanck about yesterday please fill me in pretty please tell me about yesterday I'm cumplete blanck about yesterday.

Yes, I will fill you in, come and see me immediately!

An English-speaking child writing in November of her first-grade year produced the following piece.

This is a frog. It is green. It has four legs. It is an amphibian. I like amphibians. It can hop. It can swim. I like amphibians. It sits on a lilee pad. It eats bugs. I think frogs are fun. but a frog can't fly.

All of these children had been taught spelling as outlined here. They wrote daily and were nagged to do their best. They still make mistakes in spelling but it seems evident to us that they have come to understand how to spell and find spelling so easy that they can write anything they want to say without difficulty.

Children who have been taught how to spell and who write daily almost always spell all the traditional spelling words for a given grade level with 100-percent accuracy. They usually score top marks in any standardized spelling test by getting all the words right. Something about this system works!

PART IV

What Do I Teach Monday?

As students in eighth grade, we wrote out our spelling errors fifty times, and to my adolescent horror, I often found my original errors creeping into my forty-ninth transcription. What, then, might/could/would have helped me to learn to spell those words?

Two excellent teachers describe in this section their strategies and techniques for developing spelling strengths in young people. Janice Merrifield describes her work with children, drawing upon the words they hear and read in stories as the basis for their word exploration. Larry Swartz fills his classroom with games and activities that get students working with words inside the context of puzzles and play.

Teaching Spelling with Literature
Janice Merrifield

The Ontario Ministry of Education resource document, *Education in the Primary and Junior Divisions*, states that there is little evidence that any particular method of spelling instruction produces better spellers than wide experience in reading and writing. The statement definitely makes sense, but how might it be applied in a practical way? How does spelling fit into the whole picture in a "whole language" approach to literacy development? I realized that in order to answer these questions, I had to clarify my definition of whole language. In the simplest of terms, it is the process of beginning with meaningful wholes when introducing students to the various components of language, whether reading, writing, spelling, grammar, punctuation — whatever. The answer was suddenly simple. What could be more meaningful than story, the richness of story that abounds in children's literature. And so I had found a beginning that I hoped would leave my students spellbound.

The following ideas describe a "whole language" approach to the teaching of spelling, in which the development of spelling skills occurs within the context of literary experiences, writing experiences, and specific spelling experiences. The activities can be approached in three ways:

1. Spelling instruction is *a separate component of the language arts program.*

2. Spelling instruction is *integrated into the language arts program.*

3. Spelling instruction occurs through the use of *activity centres.*

Using picture books, I will outline the three above approaches.

Amelia Bedelia by Peggy Parish (Scholastic, 1963) is an excellent book to use with late primary students. Using this story, spelling instruction can be introduced as a separate component of the language arts program, scheduled for a set time period of approximately twenty minutes per day, with activities extended over the entire school week.

Monday

Introduce the story title to the children and question them if they know anything about Amelia Bedelia. Those who are familiar with this character will be able to tell how Amelia Bedelia gets things mixed up because she has difficulty understanding what people mean. Encourage pupils to share their own experiences of getting things mixed up and what happened as a result. Read the story to the class to find out what happens to Amelia when she goes to work for the Rogers family. Discuss and share the humorous anecdotes. The students may also want to read, independently, other books from this series.

Tuesday
SKILL: WORD MEANINGS

Orally recall some of the different things that Amelia Bedelia does because she doesn't understand her instructions:

> *Change* the towels.
> *Dust* the furniture.
> Put the *light(s)* out.

Measure the rice.
Trim the fat.
Dress the chicken.

Draw attention to the first underlined word, *change*, and ask the pupils to explain the meaning of the word. Challenge them to find a different meaning for the word. Do one example co-operatively with the class.

change — to make different
      — coins (money)

Have the students write two sentences to show the double meanings. For example:

I will buy new paint to *change* the colour of the living-room.
Please make sure that you receive the correct *change* from the storekeeper.

Following the pattern of the co-operative example, have the students complete the following activity by writing two sentences to show two different meanings for each word italicized in the sentences listed above.

Wednesday

Dictate the following words (only ten to twelve words each week) to the whole class.

change	towels	draw	drapes	lights	rice
trim	dress	chicken	dust	furniture	

Collect books and mark to determine *what* difficulties students are having and *who* is having trouble. Encourage pupils to think of other expressions that would confuse Amelia Bedelia if she took them literally. List these idioms on a chart. For example:

raining cats and dogs
a frog in my throat
a green thumb
all ears
butterflies in your stomach
skipping pages

Two excellent books with similar expressions to share with the class at some time are *The King Who Rained* by Fred

Gwynne (Windmill Books, 1970) and *The Chocolate Moose* by Fred Gwynne (Windmill Books, 1976).

Thursday

Referring to the list of idioms discussed on Wednesday, have the students pretend they are Amelia Bedelia and describe orally what each idiom means in the literal sense. For example:

raining cats and dogs — cats and dogs coming down from the sky like rain

a green thumb — someone with a green-coloured thumb

After the children have started the activity, have those who had difficulty on Wednesday's dictation gather around the blackboard. Look at five or six of these words closely to help children learn how to spell them by referring to word meaning, phonics, and/or visual patterns. For example:

change — "ch" sound made by ch
     — "g" sound like "j" is called a soft "g"
     — "e" on the end is silent and makes "a" long

furniture — "ur" combination can be remembered by using the following sentence: There is cat *fur* on the *fur*niture.
     — divide into syllables
     — "ture" is like "sure"

Whenever possible, allow pupils to discover generalizations, such as noting other words that have long "a" and silent "e" (e.g., cake, mate, rake, etc.) and the variety of vowel combinations that make the "ur" sound as in fur (her, first). Expand lists with students.

Friday

Have pupils complete illustrations for idioms and neatly print the idioms on the page. Collate the pictures to create a co-operative *Amelia Bedelia Says. . .* book.

Allow five or six minutes at the end to dictate list words to the whole class. Collect and mark. Note pupils who are still having difficulty. Words should be corrected and listed below the dictation. One day in the following week, each student should be responsible for asking a friend to dictate these words to him/her. This dictation will be shared with the teacher so individual help can be given if needed.

Tales of a Gambling Grandma by Dayal Kaur Khalsa (Tundra Books, 1986) is a beautiful story to share with junior level students. It is about a little girl whose best friend is her grandma. Although they do many wonderful things together, the most wonderful thing is that grandma teaches her to play card games like poker, five-card stud, and blackjack. This sensitive and moving tale reveals how much more than cards the little girl learns from her special grandma.

Using this story, spelling instruction can be integrated into the language arts program. Many of the activities described below may be completed in one day or extended into following days based on the students' abilities, interests, and/or needs.

Before sharing this wonderful story, have the students brainstorm to list as many words as possible to describe a grandmother. Kind, loving, funny, old, wrinkled, happy, lonely, busy, youthful, patient, generous — such words are only the beginning! As these words are written down, either by the teacher or by individual students, emphasize specific spelling features wherever possible. For example:

loving — drop the silent "e" before adding "ing"
youthful — "ful" suffix meaning full of
patient — "ti" making the "sh" sound
funny — doubling a last consonant when "y" is added
generous — soft "g" sounds like "j"

Make use of these "teachable" moments to continually recognize and reinforce specific spelling skills.

Encourage the students to share personal relationships and anecdotes about their special grandma and/or other family members. This can lead into a personal writing period. Remind the students that their brainstorming words may be effective adjectives to use in their individual stories. During this writing period, preferably near the end, I would encourage the use of class conferences: one student volunteers to share his/her piece of writing with the whole class. The writer may be at any stage in the writing: beginning, middle, or end of the draft. After the reading of the selection, the other students are encouraged to make comments and/or ask questions of the writer. These questions will help the student to extend and/or clarify ideas in order to expand or carry on with the writing. Class conferences are an excellent way to model the process so that students are able to conference with each other.

Some children may wish to edit and illustrate their stories and share the published products with the class.

Tales of a Gambling Grandma also helps students discover that the English language borrows many words from other languages. Reread the sections in which grandma shares important pieces of advice which she calls her "laws of life". Here she makes reference to *borscht,* the Russian word for beet soup. Challenge the pupils to work in small groups to discover commonly used foreign words and their origin. A dictionary is a helpful resource for this activity. Some of the following are a few examples that the pupils may recall or discover:

foyer
restaurant
discotheque
tambourine   FRENCH
boutique
bouquet

kindergarten
hamburger
frankfurter   GERMAN
halt
blitz

origami
haiku
geisha   JAPANESE
bonsai
kimono

boomerang
corroboree   AUSTRALIAN ABORIGINAL

This activity may be extended into environmental studies: the students locate the countries of the above languages and choose a specific area of interest to research and share with their peers.

The above lists of words (descriptive adjectives and foreign derivatives) may be used for dictation purposes if the teacher wishes. They may also be posted in the classroom for future reference. I firmly believe that good spelling is the result of an attitude, developed through individual student commitment to writing and through effective teachers who realize that the acquisition of spelling skills is a gradual developmental process, largely dependent upon the practice of writing.

The reference to grandma's "laws of life" provides the teacher with the opportunity to discuss these examples and encourage the students to debate the issues:

> One law was all about how to draw people: Always color their cheeks bright pink and give them big red smiles so they look healthy.

> Another law was about crossing your eyes: Don't because the cords will snap and they'll stay that way forever.

> Guns are for boys. Girls play with dolls.

Throughout this study, I would display and encourage the students to read other stories that explore family relationships. The following are excellent for the junior division student:

David's Father by Robert Munsch (Annick Press, 1983)
Dinner at Auntie Rose's by Janet Munsil (Annick Press, 1984)
Love You Forever by Robert Munsch (Firefly, 1986)
The Eyes of the Amaryllis by Natalie Babbit (Bantam, 1977)
The Olden Days Coat by Margaret Laurence (McClelland & Stewart, 1979)
The Pinballs by Betsy Byars (Scholastic, 1979)
Take Wing by Jean Little (Little, Brown & Co., 1988)
A Year for Growing by Karleen Bradford (Scholastic, 1977)

The last book I will make reference to is *The Dancing Tigers* by Russell Hoban and David Gentleman (Jonathon Cape, 1979), an excellent, thought-provoking text for intermediate division students. It is the story of a wealthy Rajah, who, each year, went out hunting tigers. And each year, the tigers were aware of their fate and patiently accepted their lot. But this year it was different, for the Rajah decided to play light classics on his new stereo tape cassette player while he stalked his prey. And it was this very noise, shattering the jungle stillness, that aroused an anger in the creatures and made them decide to reveal their well-kept secret. Their secret was that they could dance, the most wonderful dances imagined. And so it was their plan to dance the Rajah to death, which they did! Presenting only the title of the book, I would encourage the student to share their predictions about "the dancing tigers" before the story is read to them. After the reading, I would provide time for them to complete the following activities, working in small groups of five or six.

Listening Centre

In a separate area, or using headphones and a tape recorder at a listening station, have the students listen to a selection of classical music. Suggested composers are Tchaikowsky, Bach, and Strauss. Challenge them to brainstorm and record as many words and phrases as possible that are inspired by the music. Co-operatively they must decide on the correct spelling of these words. Using the story and the images created by the melody, have the students move to the music and create a tableau to share with the class.

Personal Writing Centre

In the role of a palace official, have the students write a report to announce and explain the death of the Rajah. Encourage the use of peer conferencing to clarify and expand ideas.

Research Centre

Using library trade books, magazines, periodicals, and/or newspapers, have the students research animals that are still being hunted for profit or sport. Include the countries involved and the methods that are currently being used that are threatening our animal population (e.g., whales, elephants, seals). Encourage the students to debate the question of whether animals should be hunted for pleasure. They should support their opinions whenever possible, using research references.

Spelling Centre

Although the students are writing and therefore spelling at all the activity centres, I would make specific reference to the following words to reinforce dictionary skills. Challenge the students to look up the words to discover meanings and pronunciations, if needed.

Rajah (ra-je) — a Hindu prince or chief of a tribal state in India ochre (o'-ker) — a dark yellow colour

vermilion (ver-mil'-yen) — bright red colour

howdah (hou'-de) — a railed or canopied seat on the back of an elephant

mahout (me-hout') — the keeper and driver of an elephant

monogram (mon'-e-gram) — a character consisting of two or more letters interwoven into one, as the initials of several names

primitive (prim'-e-tiv) — pertaining to the beginning or origin; first; earliest

complex (kem-pleks') — complicated, involved, intricate

gilded (gil'-did) — thinly overlaid with or as with gold

sentry (sen'-try) — a soldier placed on guard to see that only authorized persons pass his post and to give warning of approaching danger

dappled (dap'-eld) — spotted

Using the text, have the students refer back to the story to clarify the meaning of each word as used in the context of *The Dancing Tigers*.

Picture-making Centre
Using the beautiful figurative language from the text, have the students illustrate a phrase or sentence to depict its meaning. Challenge the group to discuss the meanings of difficult words before they begin.

The students could complete one activity or rotate through each centre in a five-day period. This would depend on the abilities, needs, and/or interests of the students. It is important that each group have an opportunity at some time to share their products.

Although I have used children's literature as the vehicle to teach spelling, there are many ways in which we can help children to learn spelling.

How to Help Children Learn Spelling
1. Allow children many opportunities to write. It is through

the children's own writing that the most effective teaching in spelling can be done.

2. Encourage children to be risktakers. Although conventional spelling is important, it should not be allowed to inhibit the flow of writing in children. Correcting every spelling approximation with a red pencil rarely produces positive results. Children soon conclude that the less they write, the fewer mistakes they will make. The truth is just the opposite; the more they write, the fewer mistakes they will make eventually. They will never spell well if they seldom write or if, when they do, they write as little or as cautiously as possible.

3. Play spelling games which provide opportunities for students to practise word formations in challenging and enjoyable situations.

4. Create spelling lists which grow out of the current interests of the children, containing words which they are currently using. The children should select some words which they need to have on display in the classroom for reference purposes.

5. Whenever possible, help children to form generalizations. "What do you have to do to the spelling of 'stop' to write 'stopping'? Does this happen with any other words?" Generalizations that children discover stay with them.

A perfect score on a spelling test is a poor indicator of a person's real spelling behaviour. The most effective and productive spelling program is one which is rooted in a strong writing program and which acknowledges the process and developmental nature of learning to spell.

Learning Spelling through Games

Larry Swartz

Jonothan: I know I need the word *figment* because 5 down says
that the dinosaur was a _____ of his imagination. It starts
with *f*. How do you spell *figment*?

Teacher: Try it. Start with *fig*.

J: I don't know how.

T: Spel *pig*.

J: p-i-g.

T: Now spell fig.

J: p-f-i-g.

T: No, it's a three-letter word.

J: f-i-g.

T: Right! Now spell *men*, not *man*.

J: m-e-n.

T: Right! Now just add a *t*,
and you've got *figment*. Isn't spelling easy?

Miranda: I keep spelling *beautiful* wrong.

Teacher: You know, I can never remember if *address* has one
d or two. I read about this trick that helps me remember.
Watch me write this:
I will ADD your name to my ADDress book. That's how I
remember there's two *d*'s because I know *add* has two *d*'s.
Let's try a sentence to help you remember how to spell *beautiful*. Let's try *Boys eat apples under trees in fall under leaves*.
Remember that they *eat apples under trees* and you will be
able to correct -e-a-u-t.

Carson: I need a five-letter number that begins with *e*.

James: What about *eight*?

Carson: *eight* has six letters, e-i-g-h-t-e.

James: There's no *e* on the end. Now you have five letters. Just
remember there's "five in eight" and you'll leave off the *e*.

The preceding bits of dialogue are transcripts of conversations
that took place as students in my grade five class were involved
in the playing of spelling games and puzzles. Through activities that are considered to be entertaining, interesting, and creative, they were able to develop their language skills by talking

and listening and thinking about the forms and meanings of words and sentences.

This article is intended to highlight the benefits of teaching spelling through games, and to provide a list of games and activities to those teachers who want to make their spelling programs both enjoyable and meaningful.

Why Use Games to Teach Spelling?

The impulse to play games is part of every child's nature. Play is how children spend their free time as they develop their personalities and investigate their world. Their games awaken the eagerness to learn, to think, to imagine, to listen, to create, and to express ideas. Games automatically stimulate student interest. When introduced properly, a game can be one of the highest motivating techniques.

Games are basically fun-oriented and, when used in an educational context, they entertain as they motivate students to practise certain skills. When used to teach spelling, games can help overcome a child's indifference to (or even resentment of) the work involved in studying, memorizing, or reviewing words, and can possibly transform negative attitudes into a lifelong love of learning.

James Moffett and Betty Jane Wagner (1976) rationalize the use of spelling games as a good medium for learning technical aspects of language, such as phonics, spelling, homonyms, and syllabic stress, because these aspects are treated as fun. They claim that since games focus on building or recognizing isolated words, they constitute a substantial spelling program. While launching spelling, the games will, in fact, reinforce word attack and decoding without bad side effects. They are an alternative method to drill exercises or systematic spelling programs. Phonic exercises, criticized because they are allotted too much time and importance, can become dull and pointless.

Spelling games develop vocabulary, increase semantic and syntactic control, and stimulate logic and imagination. When teachers introduce spelling games into their programs, some of the teaching is indirect; that is, it simply promotes verbal facility. Thus, words that the children have seen or heard but never used themselves become parts of their active vocabulary as they play the games. Though the emphasis may be more on gaming than communicating, the meaning is never lost.

When students play games the routines of classroom drill are broken, providing fun and relaxation that remains very much within the framework of language learning — while simultaneously reinforcing that learning. Played in various forms over a number of years, games promote mental development by providing both a favourable environment for learning and the intellectual nourishment required to sustain it.

Spelling games ensure maximum student participation with a minimum of teacher preparation. At the same time, games provide immediate feedback for the teacher as students focus attention on specific structures, grammatical patterns, and vocabulary items. They can function as reinforcement, review, and enrichment of spelling rules. They involve equal participation from both slow and fast learners, and can be adjusted to suit the individual ages and language levels of the students in the class. In addition, the challenge of competition provides the children with an additional stimulus to stretch their verbal abilities as far as they can.

How to Use Spelling Games

Having justified the use of spelling games in the language class, we may then ask: "When should games be played?" and "How are they best used?" Before determining how best to introduce word games, it may be important to consider three different categories that they could fall into:

1. puzzles devised by the teacher;
2. traditional word games;
3. printed puzzles or commercial games.

1) Puzzles Devised by the Teacher

One strategy that I maintained in my program for a few months was to begin the day with a word puzzle. These puzzles were written on the board and before the national anthem was played, students were responsible for writing their answers in their "word puzzle" books. Sometimes instructions would lead the students to focus on a particular spelling rule. For instance, they might be asked to add the suffix -tion to form the words from these beginnings: *na-, rela-, concentra-, eleva-, admira-*. The words that I chose for the puzzle might come from a particular theme that we were studying (e.g., the words *height, length,* and *millimetre* were three of the puzzle words the day we studied measurement in math. Sometimes the words were drawn from errors that appeared in students' writing (e.g., *doesn't, they're, won't, couldn't*). Whether the students were asked to fill in the blank, unscramble the letters, find specific errors, or complete a word, puzzles such as the ones described later in this paper, planned by the teacher with specific objectives in mind, allowed the students to pay attention to spelling conventions and word families while playing a game.

For me, this strategy of teaching spelling benefits the students because they come to expect a study of words each day. Just as silent reading, read-aloud, and standing for "O Canada" are expected rituals in the program, daily word puzzles invite students to understand that spelling matters. It takes only a few minutes of time to write answers in their books, to interact with others at the table, and to take up the answers together. The activities also allow me to wander around the room, helping those who are struggling with a word and in this way help me to teach each speller in the classroom. Best of all, this spelling program carries over into the children's own written assignments. Often when students make errors, it is convenient to remind them of a puzzle that we studied on a particular day and make use of their puzzle books as a reference source.

Although the puzzles allowed my students to practise spelling each day, it is just one way of teaching language. After a while, the students seemed to need a break in the routine. However, before omitting these games from the daily schedule, each student was responsible for putting a word puzzle on the board for a particular day. In this way, each member of the class not only became the facilitator of an activity, but was also encouraged to pay attention to a group of "troublesome" words.

2. Traditional Word Games

Sometimes when a break in the routine of the classroom is needed, when a more relaxed activity is necessary, it is time to play a word game. I am able to select from a wide range of games that allow the students to work with partners or in small groups. The students come to have their favourite games, and for a diversion we can play one of them. The list that is provided in this article offers instructions for twenty-five games that have become personal favourites.

Generally each game that we play in the class is one that I

have played myself and, because I have understood and enjoyed the game, I can explain the rules to the class and invite them to share in the enjoyment too. I introduce most games with a short demonstration before having the entire class join in to play. For those who have difficulty following instructions it is important to have a practice so that the game runs as smoothly as possible. As children play the games, it is best to adhere to the original rules, or adjust them carefully to suit the needs of the group. If a game turns out to be too easy, the rules should be tightened or more difficult words used as examples. It is advisable to begin at an easier level before attempting to introduce any variables.

If children give up too quickly on a game, they can be encouraged or given hints. If they cannot find the answer, they should simply be told and allowed to continue. If individuals don't feel like playing a game on a particular day, they shouldn't be forced into it. They will neither enjoy nor benefit from the experience and will likely interfere with the fun others may be having. Sometimes the game may not appeal to a student, sometimes the grouping may be wrong, and sometimes the time may not be right for a game. However, before letting students choose another activity, I usually make one final attempt to play a game with them or just let them be observers or scorekeepers of a group game.

With all the games, the whole class should be involved in one way or another. This can best be realized when students choose their own groups and their own game to play. At times, several groups can be playing the same game at the same time. With other games, the whole class can be involved, the teacher acting as facilitator.

3. Printed Puzzles or Commercial Games

Many games require little more preparation than xeroxing from a book, or pulling out a box. Puzzles such as "Crosswords" and "Word Searches" are very appealing to the students. They are best used to help the students practise words on a particular theme, but they can also be used in the program to break the routines of the day. The puzzle sheets that we give to students can be played independently, but it is useful to have students interact with each other to solve the puzzles, to negotiate meaning and spelling, and to question, argue, describe, or inform together. Of course, the strategy can be extended further when students are invited to make up their own crossword or word search puzzles to share with their friends.

Several commercial games such as "Scrabble", "Boggle", "Pictionary", "Balderdash", "Probe", and "Scategories", like the puzzles and word games listed here, not only require close attention to spelling, but also provide players with the challenge of building words and stimulating vocabulary growth. As with other spelling games, many commercial games let students use words that they know, provide opportunities for students to learn new words, and encourage using the dictionary.

When choosing to introduce a game into the classroom, teachers need to consider the number of players required, the equipment or materials needed, the level of the game, and the skills or objectives that are to be taught.

It is somewhat difficult to classify the games according to age and ability level. Given any classroom, children of the same age have a different rate of intellectual growth, different exposure to verbal stimuli, and different background experiences (including experiences with games). Most games can be understood and played to accommodate varying levels of maturity. Games that prove too challenging for some may be stimulating for others. Children differ too much to fit into categories. In one sense, a spread of ages and verbal knowledge can be an advantage because "weaker" students can be helped by "stronger" students.

In promoting successful playing, it is important to consider some factors:

- noise level;
- equipment and materials needed to play the game;
- time available for the game;
- mood/tone of the class;
- curriculum being studied at the moment;
- the need for a break.

Most games that I use require few or no materials — little more than pencil and paper. Sometimes it pays to prepare equipment for a game, but time can be better spent in other ways, such as taking the time to play the game yourself. Your active participation can prove infectious to some, though others may only want to play with their peers.

Obviously, the best way to develop literacy is to read and

write real literature. The purpose of spelling games in the language arts program is ultimately to bring students to the point where they can read and write on their own. The games that children play in your classroom may become favourites that will be played outside school, with families, or even in adulthood.

For any game introduced into the program, the emphasis should always be on the play rather than on teaching. The spirit of fun should prevail to motivate and maintain students' interest. Though the games should be used to enhance language skills, the most important thing for teachers to remember is to let the games do the teaching.

Twenty-Five Games

GAME #1: NO SPACE

Write a number of words together with no spacing in between them. Then ask someone to find as many words as he or she can (a time limit can be set). Here is a sample run of words: *bookreadarkindoordeal.*

Extension: Arrange words in a circle without any spaces between the letters. Have partners list all the words they can find in the circle going clockwise. Small words that are found within bigger words can be counted separately.

GAME #2: I LOVE MY FRIEND WITH AN "A"

In this alphabet game, the first player says, "I love my friend with an A because. . ." Then, depending on the version that is decided upon, player #1 adds an adjective, or an occupation, or something that he or she likes. The next player repeats the sentence with the letter B, and so on.

Example: Player #1: I love my friend with an "A" because he/she's **adorable.**

Player #2: I love my friend with a "B" because he/she's **bold.**

GAME #3: GHOST

Several players can participate in this game. Player #1 thinks of a word and announces its first letter to the group (e.g., R). The second player, with a word in mind, adds a letter. The game continues with each player adding a letter. The object of the game is to avoid ending the word. Thus if player #2 says "e", player #3 would not say "d" (thereby spelling *red*). Players who are unable to avoid ending a word and must say the final letter, receive a letter. The first time they end a word, they receive a "G", the second time "H", the third time "O". When they have five strikes against them, they are GHOSTs and are eliminated from the game.

Players are allowed to bluff by adding a letter without actually having a word in mind. The next player in turn may challenge whether the opponent has a real word in mind and may ask for the word. If the person has bluffed, he or she gets a letter penalty (G-H-, etc.). If the first player produces a word, the challenger is penalized.

GAME #4: WORDS WITHIN WORDS

List the little words that may appear in big words. The order of the position of the letters cannot be changed. Words listed must have two or more letters — e.g., *pillow (pill, ill, low); computer (come, cot, cute, mute, comet, put, compute, cut); airplane (air, ail, are, pan, plan, plane, pane, ran, lane).*

GAME #5: ALPHABETICAL SUITCASE

A small group of players completes the sentence, "I packed my suitcase with a . . ." For this game each player must use a word that starts with the last letter of the word given by the previous player.
Example:
   Player #1: I packed my suitcase with a whal**e**.
   Player #2: I packed my suitcase with an **e**g**g**.
   Player #3: I packed my suitcase with a **g**ardenia.

GAME #6: SENTENCE IN A WORD

Partners decide upon a word of five to eight letters. Then each uses each letter of the word to start another word and create a sentence. Partners can compare answers to determine which words are similar and which sentence makes the most sense. For example: G-A-R-B-A-G-E = **G**o **a**nd **r**ead **b**ooks **a**nd **g**et **e**nlightened.

GAME #7: WORD LADDERS

With a partner, select two words of equal length and place them at the top and bottom of a "ladder" respectively. When first playing, it is recommended that three- or four-letter words be used. The top and bottom rungs of the word "ladder" could be related to each other in some way, (e.g., love-hate, city-town, hide-seek, wet-dry). The object of the game is for each player to change the first word into the second word one letter at a time, on his or her own. Each change must make a real word. The player who reaches the second word with the fewest number of changes is the winner.

Example: *stay*   *read*
            slay   *lead*
            play   *lean*
                     loan

Generally, in three-letter words, the changes are not hard to make; but with words of four or five letters, it may be necessary to make as many as a dozen or more changes to climb to the top (or down to the bottom) of the ladder.

GAME #8: WORDCHAIN

Partners or small groups create a chain of words. Player #1 writes down any word: *begin*, for example. The next person must begin the next word with the letter that ends the first word. In this case, *n*. If player #2 writes the word *never*, the next word must begin with an *r* and so on. The words are written in a continuous chain: e.g., **begineverealizenteroad**. The game could be used using a special topic such as names, cities, colours, birds.

GAME #9: LETTER SWITCH

In pairs or small groups, one player begins by saying any word that comes to mind. The next player makes a new word by changing one letter. The third player then changes one letter of the new word. The game should proceed quickly without repeating the same word twice. It is recommended that four or five letters be used for the most success.

Example: Player #1: *land*
          Player #2: *lane*
          Player #3: *sane*
          Player #4: *sang*

GAME #10: ALLITERATIVE HEADLINES

Players decide upon a letter of the alphabet. In a set time limit of five minutes, they write three-word phrases that might appear as a newspaper headline using that letter to begin each word.

For instance, for the letter *s*, the headline might read *Superman Saves Saskatchewan*. As an extension players can write longer headlines. The one with the longest headline is the "winner".

GAME #11: TELEGRAMS

In groups of five or six, each player needs a piece of paper and a pencil. Each player in turn says any letter of the alphabet. As each letter is given, it is written down on a piece of paper in the order in which it is called out. Once all the letters are written down, each player must compose a telegram using each letter as the first letter of a new word. For example, the letters *FCSMIMBOPD* might become *Found clue. Send memo in morning. Beware of pink dinosaurs*. Players should try to compose messages that make some kind of sense, however strange they may sound.

GAME #12: WHAT'S MY WORD?

In pairs, each player thinks of a word that consists of an agreed-upon number of letters. Each then writes on a piece of paper as many dashes as there are letters in the word. Player #1 chooses a letter of the alphabet and inquires whether the letter is in the opponent's word. If it is, the second player must write the letter over the dash that represents it and show this to the first player. If the letter is used more than once in the word, it must be written wherever it occurs. The first player, seeing the letter written in one or more spaces on the opponent's paper, continues asking about other letters until the letter called out is not in the word.

Player #2 then takes a turn to ask about the letters in the first player's word. The game continues in this way until one of the players successfully guesses the word of the other from seeing its letters gradually filled in.

GAME #13: CHOOSY CHARLES

In groups, one person begins by announcing: "I am choosing a gift for Choosy Charles who detests *e*'s. What will you give Choosy Charles?"

Each player, in turn, names a gift for Choosy Charles that does not have the letter *e* in it. If a player names a gift that has already been mentioned or that contains the letter *e*, he or she is eliminated.

Player #1: I will give Choosy Charles a *lamp*.
Player #2: I will give Choosy Charles a *candy*.
Player #3: I will give Choosy Charles a *flower*.
Leader: You're out! flower has an *e*.

The game can be repeated by naming other letters that Choosy Charles does not like. For instance, he may not like *b*'s, *c*'s, *i*'s, *l*'s, *p*'s, or *t*'s. The leader decides upon a specific vowel that Choosy Charles does not like, or names two letters that must be avoided.

GAME #14: WORD RACE

Groups of five or six sit in a circle. Player #1 names a letter (excluding *xyz*) of the alphabet — *l*, for example. On a signal, the player on the right must, within one minute, name as many words as he or she can think of that begin with that letter. As the words are called — lemon, lamp, licence, leader, etc. — the first player counts them while keeping track of the time. Plurals, repetitions, or variations of the same word are not acceptable.

When a minute is up, the second player is given one point for each word he or she named. Then it is player #2's turn to time the player on the right for another letter of the alphabet. The game proceeds in this way until all players have taken a turn, each with a different letter. The one who gets the most words wins the game.

The game can be made more challenging by setting a rule that the words be of two syllables, three syllables, or five letters or more than five letters.

GAME #15: ANTONYMS AND SYNONYMS

In a group, the first player calls out a word — almost any word will do — although adjectives are probably the easiest to handle. The second player gives an antonym of that word, the third player a synonym for the second player's word, the fourth player an antonym of the third player's word, and so on. If stuck, a player may use a rhyming word.

Example: Player #1: hot
Player #2: cold
Player #3: cool
Player #4: warm
Player #5: fresh

Player #6: stale
Player #7: pale (rhyme)
Player #8: vivid

GAME #16: CATEGORIES

Two or more people can play this game. First, each player is asked in turn to name a category such as flowers, fruit, countries, celebrities, fish, trees, authors, cars, etc. As these are named, each player lists them vertically on a sheet of paper.

The group agrees on a five-letter word, such as *watch*. This is written across the top of each player's page. Each player then makes a rectangular chart with boxes large enough to accommodate the words to be filled in.

A ten-minute time limit is given, and on a signal each player has to fill in the boxes by finding in every category a word that begins with the letter at the top of the column.

For instance, a completed chart might look like this.

	W	A	T	C	H
TREES	walnut	ash	tulip	cedar	hickory
TOOLS	wrench	axe	t-square	compass	hammer
GIRLS' NAMES	Wendy	Ann	Theresa	Cindy	Helen
BIRDS	wren	albatross	tern	cockatoo	heron
FLAVOURS	walnut	almond	tomato	chocolate	herb

Once the game is finished, papers are exchanged for scoring. A point could be given for each word that appropriately suits the category.

An alternate way of scoring may be more challenging. A player reads aloud the first word on the paper he or she is scoring. If the word is correct, the player who thought of it receives as many points as there are other players who did *not* have it on their papers. Thus, if five are playing the game and only one thought of *albatross*, that word would be worth four points; but if two players had thought of it, each of them would be credited with three points for it. The same procedure is followed with each word and the player who scores the most points wins.

GAME #17: SPELL A CATEGORY

Two teams of five or six players are needed. Each player in turn draws, from a box or bag, a letter printed on a card and spells a word that both begins with this letter and belongs to a previously selected category, such as street names, capital cities, bodies of water. If the player does not give an acceptable word, or misspells it, a player on the opposing team gets a chance. One point is given for each acceptable word that is spelled correctly.

GAME #18: HOW MANY WORDS CAN YOU BUILD?

A long word is decided upon, such as *neighbourhood*, *caterpillar*, or *valentines*. The players can compete to see how many new words of three letters or more they can spell rearranging the letters of the word. A letter can be used only as many times as it appears in the word. The player (or pair of players) with the most words wins the game. Or scoring can be given for words that are three letters, four letters, five letters long, etc. Example: *valentines — leave, veil, snail, invent, save,* etc.

GAME #19: VANISHING VOWELS

Write a simple sentence removing all the vowels. Exchange with a partner and try to reconstruct the original sentence: Here's an example: *Spelling games can be lots of fun.*

sp-ll-ng g-m-s c-n b- l-ts -f f-n

To make the game more challenging you can eliminate the dashes so that the puzzle would look like this: *spllng gms cn b fn.*

GAME #20: JOTTO

Play this game for partners with a piece of paper and a pencil. The object of the game is to guess the five-letter word that the other player is thinking of while that player is trying to guess your own secret word at the same time. The first player to guess the other's secret word is the winner.

Each player writes down a five-letter word on the top of the page and hides that word from the partner. It is recommended that all the letters in the words be different, and that there be no double consonants or vowels.

Players take turns guessing which five-letter word they think the other player has written down. Each player, in turn, gives the opponent a five-letter word that he or she writes down. The opponent tells his or her partner how many letters in this word are in their word. Don't say which letters, just how many are correct. For instance, if your word is *flows* and your partner calls out *grows*, you say that three letters in *grows* are also in your word. Players take turns calling out five-letter words.

At the bottom of the sheet of paper write out the alphabet. If you guess a word that has no letters in your partner's word, cross out the letters in the alphabet that are in the word you guessed. If you discover by elimination that a letter definitely appears in the five-letter word, circle it in the alphbet. Keep trying until you guess all five letters and can solve the puzzle.

Here is what a game of JOTTO might look like.

Flows

Players guess:

GROWS — 3

GREAT — 0 (player can cross out g-r-e-a-t from the alphabet and therefore has quickly discovered that three of the letters are *o w s*, since *g* and *r* must be eliminated from *grows*)

BROWN — 2

FROWN — 3

GAME #21: SPELLING DUEL

This game is a spelling bee for two players. Each is given a list of ten words that are equally difficult. Player #1 begins by calling a word to the opponent, challenging him or her to spell the word correctly in ten seconds. Two points are given for each correct spelling.

Players take turns, alternately calling out a word from their lists. When all twenty words have been completed, the "duellists" exchange "swords" — i.e., their lists of words. This time one point is given for each correct spelling. The players keep exchanging the lists until both spell every word correctly within the allotted time. The player who accumulates the greatest number of points wins the game.

The game can be made more challenging by making the lists longer or by including more difficult words.

GAME #22: HANGMAN

Working in a pair, player #1 chooses a word (which can be a name or title) and on a piece of paper puts the number of dashes that the word contains. The opponent guesses one letter at a time, eventually trying to guess the word. If the guess is correct, player #1 fills in each dash that contains that letter. Each time players call a letter that is not in the word, they are penalized with a body part, taking a step toward "hanging" themselves, first the head, and then in turn, the body, each arm, each leg, each eye, the mouth, and the nose. The object, of course, is to avoid being "hanged".

GAME #23: WORD PYRAMIDS

Verbal pyramids are built from the top down. They start with the apex, which consists of a single letter — the same for all players. Each player then works independently, adding one letter at a time to make new words, rearranging previously used letters if necessary. These new words are listed below the original letter to form a pyramid. The player who writes down the most words in a given amount of time wins the game — counting only those words that are spelled correctly. Here is an example of how two players might form pyramids starting with the letter "i":

i	i
it	it
mit (incorrect)	kit
timer	knit
merits	think
	knight
	knights

The game can be made more difficult if the players are not allowed to change the order of the letters from word to word.

GAME #24: PING PONG WORDS

This game is played in pairs with players taking turns calling out words as fast as they can to see how many they can complete before time is up. (Suggested time: two minutes.) An egg timer can be used to time the game. A third player might time the players and be the caller who begins by asking, "How many words can you name that have . . . [e.g.] double letters? Go!"

The game might begin with player #1 calling out *address* and the second *dribble*, and continue at a fast pace with such words as *umbrella, well, wrapped, jazz*, etc. until the timer stops.

The game can be made more challenging by having the caller ask for specific letters, such as double vowels only, or double *t*'s, or by reviewing prefixes (*mis, pre, dis, re*), suffixes (*ize, ious, al*), or endings (*ology, able, ible, ism, itis*).

The timer can list the number of words that were given and challenge another group to beat the score.

GAME #25: THE MINISTER'S CAT

Any number of players can play this game, perhaps sitting in a circle. Each player, in turn, calls out, "The minister's cat is a(n) . . . cat". The first player fills in the blank with an adjective beginning with an *a* (e.g., *a*dorable, *a*dventurous, *a*ffectionate). Player #2 must describe the cat with a *b* adjective, and so on throughout the alphabet. It is important to keep the rhythm of the chant going. To make the game challenging and fun, the beat must not be broken or slowed down. Clapping can be done to maintain the rhythm.

This game can be extended by setting up other spelling rules for the adjectives that describe the cat (e.g., words must all end in *y*/can only be two syllables, etc.).

Selected Bibliography

Golick, Margie, Ph.D. (1987). *Playing with Words*. Toronto: Pembroke Publishers Limited.

Hurwitz, Abraham B., and A. Goddard (1969). *Games to Improve Your Child's English*. Simon and Schuster.

Kohl, Herbert (1981). *A Book of Puzzlements*. New York: Schocken Books.

McCallum, George P. (1980). *101 Word Games*. New York: Oxford University Press.

Moffet, James, and Betty Jane Wagner (1983). *Student-Centered Language Arts and Reading, K-13: A Handbook for Teachers*. Boston: Houghton Mifflin Company.

Robson, Ann and John (1974). *Word Games for Families Who Are Still Speaking to Each Other*. Don Mills, Ontario: Paperjacks.

PART V

Does Spelling Count?

In public school, I received a dollar from my father for every "A" on my report card. One slip in spelling meant a drop in my marks and my funds. What a strange way to assess word power!

Kristine Anderson has developed helpful spelling surveys to assess the strategies and errors of students in the older grades. Ruth Scott presents her philosophy for developing a comprehensive spelling assessment program for children.

Using a Spelling Survey to Assess Students' Strategies and Errors

Dr. Kristine F. Anderson

Recently there has been a great deal of interest in children's invented spellings and their spelling errors. Studies indicate that misspellings are seldom random or haphazard, but instead very systematic and logical (Ganchow, 1983; Gentry, 1978, 1981; Henderson & Beers, 1977; Read, 1971; Shaughnessy, 1977; Zutell, 1979). An analysis of students' spelling errors provides valuable information about their understanding of the writing system and their writing behavior. Errors reflect the system of rules and strategies students draw on while composing (Barrit & Kroll, 1978) as well as their developmental stage.

Although many error analyses have been developed over the years (Spache, 1940; Shaughnessy, 1977; Conley, 1974; Lyons, 1986), the time-honored approach is product-oriented. Most analyses treat spelling as a discrete skill and focus on the number and type of errors students make. Few have attempted to consider students' spelling strategies in the context of the writing process or their understanding of the writing system.

To provide information about older students' spelling ability and the developmental nature of written language competence, however, an examination of errors must go beyond a study of the omission and insertion of letters. An examination of errors must be based on the current research into English orthography and the spelling process to plan appropriate instruction.

A simple yet effective approach involves using an informal survey that helps students analyze their strategies and errors qualitatively to determine the cause of their errors. When students analyze their strategies and look for a pattern in their errors, they begin to see the "logic of their mistakes" (Shaughnessy, 1977). More importantly, they learn to control their errors and develop a variety of effective strategies that improve their fluency.

Before discussing the survey further, however, it will be helpful to briefly discuss the writing system and the developmental nature of the spelling process.

The Nature of the Writing System and the Development of Spelling Ability

Historically, the English writing system has been viewed as an illogical and often confusing means of representing the sounds of language. Research (Chomsky & Halle, 1968) shows, however, that the writing system is a highly complex but regular system that represents linguistic information at the levels of sound, meaning, and syntax. The regularity is based on underlying meaning units, or lexical items, rather than sound units.

While English spelling represents sounds to some degree, it more consistently represents structural patterns and the underlying meanings of words (Becker et al., 1980). Indeed, many words that are similar in meaning are similar in spelling. Predictable phonetic variations are not usually represented in order to maintain the meaning connection among related words. To illustrate, although the word pair "courage" and "courageous" differ phonetically, they are similar in spelling.

Learning to spell is no longer considered to be a mechanistic activity involving the memorization of a long list of sound-letter correspondence rules and their exceptions. Nor is it simply a matter of practice and drill. Instead, learning to spell is a "highly complex intellectual accomplishment" (Hodges, 1981).

Like other language-based activities, learning to spell is a developmental process marked by specific stages. The development of spelling ability is closely related to the acquisition of a complex rule system and a variety of strategies for processing written language as a multilevel system. Children gradually internalize information about the underlying rules, construct tentative rules of their own, and then apply those rules as they write (Henderson, 1981).

Children do not have a conscious understanding of the complexity of the writing system when they first pick up paper and pencil. When they begin to experiment with writing, they rely on letter sound information and are quite proficient in sounding words out (Read, 1971). As they gain more experience with print, they develop a more integrated view of the writing system and increasingly sophisticated strategies.

Marsh et al. (1980) found that in spelling, as well as in reading, "the more experienced subjects switch from a phomemic encoding strategy to a strategy based on analogy with known words in the visual memory". They recognized that using a phonemic strategy would result in errors when spelling polysyllabic words with reduced syllables and/or silent letters. At about age ten, use of the analogy strategy appears to increase as children's store of visual word forms increases. Instead of decoding an unfamiliar word, they search for a known word and pronounce or spell the unfamiliar word by analogy to it. To illustrate, when asked to spell nonsense words which were lexically related and structurally similar to real words, as in "cuscle"/"cuscular" (muscle/muscular), Marsh et al. found that the use of analogies increased as subjects' grade level increased.

When Frith (1980) studied the errors and strategies of three groups of middle school aged children — good readers/good spellers; good readers/poor spellers; and poor readers/poor spellers — she found a difference in the errors and strategies. Good readers/good spellers used a combination of strategies, including semantic or structural analogies, and drew on rules based on deep levels of linguistic analysis.

Very few studies have been done on the errors and strategies of older students. However, an informal study done by Gould (1976) and a study done by Coughlan (1980) supports research conducted by Frith (1980) and Marsh et al. (1980) on the developmental shift that occurs in good spellers between second grade and college. Gould found that good adult spellers operated with some implicit rule system when predicting the spelling of a nonsense word which was structurally similar to a real word. They appeared to capitalize on their knowledge of the real word. Coughlan (1980) reported that when spelling nonsense words college students tended to rely on a visual analogy strategy which reflected rules for consonant doubling and vowel alternation. They appeared to draw on patterns represented by real words administered earlier on the same test.

Anderson (1982) concluded that college students who are good readers/good spellers use more varied and sophisticated strategies than do poor readers/poor spellers when spelling four complex word patterns with a change in pronunciation and stress, as in "inspire"/"inspiration". In subsequent research (1987), I found that college students who are poor spellers made errors which reflected confusion about meaning-sound relationships. When spelling derived forms, such as "competition", they relied on how the word sounded. Apparently unaware of the underlying root word, they omitted letters or substituted inappropriate letters for the schwa, or reduced vowel. For example, one student wrote: *relitives* (relatives); *opertunities* (opportunities); and *monatary* (monetary). Some of the students also made errors when spelling homonym forms as well as errors which seemed to result from a lack of visual information. For example, one student wrote: *apeal* (appeal) and *further more* (furthermore). Like Frith, I concluded that they have not made the qualitative shift to higher level strategies which draw on underlying levels of linguistic information.

In light of the above descriptions of the writing system and research, it is possible to consider some spelling difficulties in terms of limited linguistic knowledge of the different levels of the writing system as well as limited strategies (Frith, 1979). Poor spellers seem to be locked into a limited number of strategies which rely on phonological, or surface level information. Like beginning writers, they see the writing system as one-dimensional, with strict one-to-one correspondence. They often lack an understanding of the morphemic and syntactic constraints placed on English spelling.

Indeed, many poor spellers are unaware of using any type of strategy at all. They often consider correct spelling to be a matter of luck and chance. They are, as Shaugnessy notes, bewildered by their graphemic options, particularly when trying to spell polysyllabic words. Often, they cannot distinguish a correctly spelled word from an incorrect word. In addition, many poor spellers are unaware of their error patterns because they are unaware of the underlying patterns in the writing system. Although instructors regularly mark "SP", students continue making the same errors week after week.

Design and Use of the Survey

Rather than simply asking students to correct their errors and drill, instructors must help them consider their error patterns as well as the underlying processes involved in accurate spelling. Since correct spelling requires a high degree of linguistic skill and a combination of strategies (Ganchow, 1983), the first five items on the survey focus on different strategies used by effective spellers: sound information; rules; analogies — or words related in meaning or structure; the dictionary; and visual information.

The sixth and seventh questions focus on proofreading, or self-correcting strategies used during the editing stage of writing. The last questions focus on an error classification scheme which involves eight general categories of words that often prove troublesome for poor spellers: 1) words with silent letters; 2) words with unstressed vowels or schwas; 3) words with prefixes; 4) words with suffixes; 5) words with Latin or Greek roots; 6) homonym forms; 7) common words and phrases, including transitions; 8) miscellaneous words. (The categories were determined during a preliminary study which analyzed the spelling errors of fifty-five basic writers enrolled in a developmental English course during the fall quarter in 1983. While there are other categories that could have been used, the above are relatively easy for students to identify).

INDIVIDUAL SPELLING SURVEY

	ALWAYS	FREQUENTLY	OCCASIONALLY	NEVER
1. Do you try to spell words the way you think they sound?				
2. Do you try to use spelling rules when appropriate?				
3. If you cannot spell a word, do you consider the meaning or structure of the word?				
4. If you cannot spell a word, do you consider the meaning of a related word or a word in the same family?				
5. Do you use a dictionary or wordbook rather than a thesaurus?				
6. Can you tell if a word you've written doesn't "look right"?				
7. Do you take time to proofread specifically for spelling errors as you write?				
8. Do you take time to proofread specifically for spelling errors as you edit?				
9. Do you frequently misspell the same words?				
10. Do you notice any pattern in your misspelled words?				
a. words with silent letters				
b. words with unstressed vowels (ə)				
c. words with prefixes				
d. words with suffixes				
e. words with a Latin or Greek root				
f. homonym forms				
g. common words and phrases, including transitions				
h. miscellaneous words				

Students should complete the survey after they have written two or three papers and listed all of their errors. The instructor may wish to distribute the survey, or part of it, at the end of the quarter to check the students' progress. Since the survey is designed to encourage self-assessment and error analysis, students simply check the appropriate column under ALWAYS, FREQUENTLY, OCCASIONALLY, and NEVER.

After instructors have helped students complete the survey, instructors can plan appropriate activities. To illustrate, students who frequently misspell words with silent letters and unstressed vowels are likely trying to spell words "the way they sound". Like young writers, they are relying on sound-letter correspondences, or surface level information. They are not aware of the morphological principles and underlying patterns inherent in the writing system.

Instructors can help students understand the logic of silent letters, though, by pointing out the role of silent letters in maintaining the meaning connection between related words. For example, the silent "b" in bomb is pronounced in "bombard." As students make connections between related words with silent letters, they learn a key principle in English spelling — *spelling reflects meaning*. They begin to develop higher level strategies and a systematic means of dealing with vocabulary (Chomsky, 1970). More importantly, they begin to identify patterns, so they can make some appropriate generalizations about the pattern principles in the writing system.

Many poor spellers who rely on sound make a variety of errors when spelling words with affixes because they are unfamiliar with the basic structure or "carpentry of words" (Shaughnessy, 1977). Words with a suffix are particularly troublesome, especially when the addition of a suffix results in a change in pronunciation, as in "divine" and "divinity". Such students need systematic instruction in making connections between related words and frequent patterns, such as "console" and "consolation", where a long vowel is shortened with the addition of the suffix. They also need instruction in patterns involving a change in pronunciation and stress of a derivative, such as "explain" and "explanation", where there is a change in both the pronunciation and the spelling.

Students who misspell words with affixes also seem to have problems with spelling rules. Indeed, some are unaware that there are rules for affixation. Others either fail to use appropriate rules and/or overgeneralize rules. They need explicit instruction in some of the frequently used rules concerning affixation, such as the rules for maintaining the base of a word when adding a prefix and the rule for keeping the final "e" when adding a suffix beginning with a consonant. It is important, however, to emphasize the application of appropriate rules in meaningful writing rather than in rote memorization tasks.

Since many poor spellers are also poor readers with limited vocabularies, they often pull words from a thesaurus and produce stilted papers. Instruction should extend students' existing vocabularies by presenting some information on the history of the writing system as well as the meaning of more commonly occurring Latin and Greek roots and combining forms. For example, instructors can present some of the more frequently used Latin roots, such as "duct" — to lead; "fac," "fic" — to make; and "mis," "mit" — to send. Instructors may, however, wish to introduce students to the Greek numerical prefixes first since they are easier to isolate and identify than many of the Latin roots.

Students who misspell homonym forms concentrate on sound, or phonological information. They would benefit from a review of homonyms and commonly confused words to become more aware of the use of context and syntactic information in selecting the appropriate form. The use of mnemonics might also be helpful in distinguishing between different forms (e.g., "the word *dessert* has two *s*'s because it's super sweet").

Common words and phrases, including transitions, are another source of frequent errors for poor spellers. Since they usually do very little reading, they do not develop a memory for correct forms. They join or separate words and phrases in unconventional ways, producing the following types of errors: *eventhough* (even though) and *further more* (furthermore). In addition, they do not attend to the sequence of letters, so they frequently transpose letters. They make the following type of errors — *certian* (certain) and *esle* (else).

Since visual information is an important aspect of accurate spelling and the development of effective strategies (Barron, 1980; Frith, 1980; Marsh et al., 1980; Simon and Simon, 1973), instructors must help students "retrain their eyes" (Shaughnessy, 1977) and improve their visual memory. Instructors can encourage students to make flash cards of words they consistently misspell. Students can then review the cards so they can produce the correct forms in their writing.

Finally, many poor spellers make numerous errors because of poor and/or inappropriate proofreading habits which reflect a breakdown in the composing process. They try to correct as they write and become hypercorrectors, developing a "stop 'n' go" writing style (Perl, 1979). To become fluent writers, however, they must learn to separate the production and revising process from the proofreading process.

Accordingly, instructors need to provide students with the time and opportunities to become more reflective writers, so they can develop self-correcting strategies. Indeed, proofreading is a highly developed skill difficult for even experienced writers and good spellers. Many students may spell a word correctly in the title of a paper and incorrectly in the conclusion simply because they "ran out of time". Instructors can encourage students to lightly mark or circle words they think are incorrect, so they can check those words when they proofread. They can also demonstrate specific proofreading techniques that help students recognize their errors.

One of the most effective techniques involves moving the edge of a half-piece of paper or a three-by-five card with a slit cut in the middle down the page as one reads. Using a paper or card forces students to slow down and attend to individual letters or words rather than reading in chunks. Another effective technique involves pairing students up, so they can proofread their papers aloud to their partners, or even exchange papers.

Students must acquire a "sense of doubt" that will motivate them to check the dictionary or wordbook when they are unsure of a spelling. They may, though, need instruction on how to use the dictionary, particularly in trying to find words they have no idea how to spell.

In summary, traditional methods of error analysis and spelling remediation often prove frustrating for both students and their teachers. However, an informal analysis of the strategies and the spelling errors made during the composing process can be helpful in assessing students' understanding of the writing system as well as the source of their difficulties. Using the survey can help students determine their dominant strategies and develop more effective strategies to limit their errors.

Works Cited

Anderson, Kristine. "An Analysis of the Spelling Errors Made by Three College Students in Essay Writing." *Journal of Research and Development in Education* 20 (1987): 40-50.

_____. "The Spelling Errors and Strategies of College and Adult Spellers." *Innovative Learning Strategies 1983-84.* Commerce, TX: College Reading Improvement Special Interest Group, International Reading Association (1984): 63-73.

_____. *The Spelling Errors and Strategies of College Students Who Are Good Readers/Good Spellers and College Students Who Are Poor Readers/Poor Spellers on Four Complex Word Patterns.* Unpublished doctoral dissertation, Georgia State University (1982).

Barrit, L.S., and Barry Kroll. "Some Implications of Cognitive Developmental Psychology for Research in Composing." Eds. Charles Cooper and Lee O'Dell, *Research in Composing: Points of Departure.* Urbana, Ill: National Council of Teachers of English (1978).

Barron, Roderick. "Visual and Phonological Strategies in Reading and Spelling." Ed. Uta Frith, *Cognitive Processes in Learning to Spell.* London: Academic Press (1980): 195-215.

Becker, Wesley, Robert Dixon, and Lynne Anderson-Inman. "Morphological and Root Word Analysis of 26,000 High Frequency Words." Eugene, OR: U of Oregon (1980). Grant No. G00-7507234.

Chomsky, Carol. "Reading, Writing, and Phonology." *Harvard Educational Review* 40 (1970): 278-309.

Chomsky, Noam, and Morris Halle. *The Sound Patterns of English.* New York: Harper (1968).

Conley, James. "Speling." *College Composition and Communication* 25 (1974): 243-246.

Coughlan, Georgiana. "Spelling: Rules versus Learning Strategies. San Francisco: Western College Reading Association (1980). ERIC Document Reproduction Service No. ED 189 579.

Frith, Uta. "Annotation." *Journal of Child Psychology and Psychiatry and Allied Difference* 20 (1979): 279-294.

_____. "Unexpected Spelling Problems." Ed. Uta Frith. *Cognitive Processes and Learning to Spell.* London: Academic Press (1980): 495-517.

Ganchow, Lenora. "Trends: Spelling Research." *Reading News* 12 (1983): 1-2.

Gentry, J. Richard. "Early Spelling Strategies." *The Elementary School Journal* 79 (1978): 88-92.

_____. "Learning to Spell Developmentally." *The Reading Teacher* 34 (1981): 378-83.

Gould, Sandra. "Spelling Isn't Reading Backwards." *Journal of Reading* 20 (1976): 220-225.

Henderson, Edmund. *Learning to Read and Spell: the Child's Knowledge of Words.* Dekalb, Ill: Northern Illinois University Press (1981).

Henderson, Edmund, and James Beers. "A Study of Developing Orthographic Concepts among First Graders." *Research in Teaching English* 11 (1977): 134-148.

Hodges, Richard. *Learning to Spell.* Urbana, Ill: National Council of Teachers of English (1982).

Lyons, C. "Spelling Inventory." *Journal of Basic Writing* Spring 5 (1986): 80-84.

Marsh, George, Morton Friedman, Veronica Welch, and Peter Desberg, "The Development of Strategies in Spelling." Ed. Uta Frith, *Cognitive Processes and Learning How to Spell.* London: Academic Press, (1980): 333-355.

Perl, Sondra. "The Composing Processes of Unskilled Writers." *Research in the Teaching of English* 13 (1979): 316-336.

Read, Charles. "Pre-school Children's Knowledge of Phonology." *Harvard Educational Review* 41 (1971): 1-34.

Shaughnessy, Mina. *Errors and Expectations.* New York: Oxford Press (1977).

Simon, Dorthea, and Herbert Simon. "Alternative Uses of Phonemic Information in Spelling." *Review of Educational Research* 43 (1973): 115-137.

Spache, George. "Characteristic Errors of Good and Poor Spellers." *Journal of Educational Research* 34 (1940): 182-189.

Templeton, W. Shane. "Using the Spelling/Meaning Connection to Develop Word Knowledge in Older Students." *Journal of Reading* (1983): 8-14.

Zutell, Jerry. "Spelling Strategies of Primary School Children and Their Relationship between Orthography and Higher Order Phonology in Older Students." *Research in the Teaching of English* 13 (1979): 255-64.

Spelling Assessment: The Missing Link

Ruth Scott

A great deal has been learned in recent years about the nature of the English spelling system and the processes involved in learning to spell. Rather than viewing the spelling system as random and chaotic, linguists now stress the patterns underlying our written language. In a similar fashion, children are no longer seen as interacting with English spelling in a haphazard manner, but instead are observed making increasingly sophisticated inferences about the patterns of written English. These new perspectives on language and language learning have led to fundamental changes in how spelling is addressed in classrooms. Rote memorization has given way to approaches which stress the formation of concepts about written English and the application of these observations to everyday writing. The child is seen as an active participant in the quest to make sense of the English spelling system.

Ironically, the advances made in the teaching of spelling have often not been carried over to the assessment of spelling skills. In many classrooms, students continue to receive standardized spelling tests which can be converted to grade scores. These results are then used as the sole basis for grouping children for instruction. In other classrooms, no assessment procedures are used for spelling, other than very general observations based on the children's personal writing. In both instances, a wealth of information which could be used to help students progress smoothly toward conventional spelling is overlooked.

In order for spelling assessment to be consistent with current knowledge of linguistics and spelling development, a number of principles should underlie the procedures selected.

1. Assessment Strategies Should be Viewed as "Windows" into the Child's Mind

All too often, spelling assessment has focused on the number of errors committed by the child, either in a dictated test or in the context of the child's writing. Such procedures, while providing general information about spelling achievement, are very narrow in their scope. More often than not, they reveal what the child *cannot* do, but provide little insight into why. A more productive approach is to focus on what the child does not know about the spelling system and what logic the child is using in making decisions about spelling.

The following case illustrates the benefits of providing a positive orientation to spelling assessment. A grade seven student, who was involved in a research study I was conducting on spelling, had been given a standardized spelling test as a screening measure. The results of the test showed his spelling skills to be in the twenty-fifth percentile for his age group, at least two years below grade level. When I met with him to discuss his perceptions of his spelling skills, he revealed a very low opinion of himself as a speller and was clearly uncomfortable. Rather than confirming his self-assessment with the test results, I chose to show him some of his errors and to discuss the reasons he may have had for selecting these spellings. In each case, I recopied the portion of each word that was spelled corrcctly and left a blank space for each incorrect letter. I congratulated him on the fact that most of the letters were correctly spelled; we then focused on the one or two misspelled letters in each word.

The examples selected are as follows:

Key Word	Student's Attempt	
political	palitical	p__litical
campaign	campain	campai__n
community	comunity	com__unity
continuity	contenuety	cont__nu__ty
tangible	tangable	tang__ble

It was soon apparent that the boy's errors were not the result of a "terminal" case of spelling dysfunction. By focusing on what he *could* do, I found that he had a good grasp of sound/symbol principles and was able to produce the correct number of syllables in each word. His problem was that he relied too heavily on a phonetic approach to spelling, and was, therefore, unable to deal with silent letters (campaign), double consonants (community), and schwa vowels (vowels in unstressed syllables, as in tangible). Once the student realized that he had mastered a significant portion of the spelling system (the sound level), but needed to enrich his spelling strategies to encompass more complex spelling patterns and visual features, his attitude improved remarkably. My suggestions for improving his spelling were based on a logical approach which addressed his specific needs. He no longer felt victimized by the spelling system.

2. The Child Should Be Actively Involved in the Assessment

Spelling assessments have traditionally been conducted without any meaningful involvement on the part of the child. The dictated spelling test and samples of writing are like blood samples taken in a medical laboratory, sent out for analysis, and assigned either positive or negative results. In the case of a poor speller, a course of treatment is prescribed which may or may not have any logical connection with the nature of the child's spelling difficulties. This "medical model" of spelling assessment not only neglects the active involvement of the primary source of information, the child, but it also deprives the child of a sense of ownership in the findings.

To encourage that sense of ownership, a discussion concerning spelling may take place in the context of an editing conference focusing on a specific piece of writing, or as a separate conversation concerning the child's experiences with spelling. A number of avenues may be pursued depending on the child's age and level of comfort. Since spelling is related to a variety of other language skills, a broad range of issues should be explored. Some of them are described below.

The Child's Self-Image as a Speller

Some children are aware of their strengths and weaknesses as spellers and are open to suggestions for improvement. Others see themselves as hopelessly poor spellers and often feel a sense of hostility towards spelling assistance. These children must be helped to realize that there is usually a logical reason for their spelling errors. They can then be shown strategies for overcoming these problems in a systematic fashion.

Previous Spelling Instruction

Children in any given class will vary widely in the nature of spelling instruction they have encountered. Some will have experienced an informal spelling program which addresses spelling needs as they arise. Others will have participated in a formal approach to spelling involving the use of spelling texts, regular dictations, and so forth. It is important to be aware of these factors, since students who appear to be lagging behind in spelling skills may simply lack the experience of looking at spelling patterns and utilizing spelling strategies when faced with unfamiliar words. Another possibility is that previous instructional strategies for spelling may have been inappropriate for the needs of a particular student. A heavy focus on phonics, for example, would be ineffective for a student who is having difficulty recalling the visual features of words.

The Child's Interests and Skills in Reading and Writing

Although not all good readers are good spellers, the two skill areas share many of the same components. Children who do not read on a regular basis are limiting their opportunities to encounter words in print which they could use in their own writing. They are also depriving themselves of chances to make hypotheses about the spelling system based on frequently occurring patterns in their reading. It is helpful to listen to their oral reading, since difficulties in decoding words may suggest inadequate knowledge of sound/symbol principles, which in turn may affect the ability to apply such principles to the spelling of words.

Determining a child's attitude toward personal writing may also provide useful information in the assessment of spelling skills. Children who lack the opportunity or desire to write on a regular basis will have fewer chances to experiment with the spelling system and apply the patterns they may have observed in reading to their own writing. Such children may also have little motivation to improve their spelling, since the connection between accurate spelling and the editing of a final draft will not be apparent.

The Child's Ability to Use a Variety of Strategies when Spelling Unfamiliar Words

Many poor spellers use a narrow range of strategies when learning to spell new words. They may, for example, write out each word several times without any attempt to focus on specific features of the word, or they may simply read the word aloud. Such students need to develop a repertoire of spelling strategies and be able to select the appropriate strategy for learning a given word. For example, a visual approach would be most effective in studying words which contain silent letters, schwa vowels, or unusual spelling patterns. On the other hand, paying attention to auditory features may be the most efficient way of handling words which contain familiar sound/symbol patterns. An application of knowledge concerning base words, prefixes, and suffixes would be a logical strategy when faced with a word such as "international". Cooperative learning groups are an excellent vehicle for helping students develop a variety of approaches to spelling, since children can benefit from the strategies of other members of the group.

Students should also be encouraged to utilize their natural learning styles with spelling tasks. While they need to possess a variety of spelling strategies, they will likely develop preferred styles for studying words. Helping children to become aware of their natural preferences may be an important component of spelling assessments.

The Logic the Child Uses in Generating a Spelling for a Specific Word

When the teacher analyzes a child's spelling, a number of hypotheses may be generated concerning the child's choice of letters. It is often fruitful, however, to have the student verbalize the reasons underlying these choices as the writing is taking place. Such discussions may help to reveal the child's understanding of the spelling system and suggest a direction for further growth.

Teachers are often surprised by the logic underlying apparently random choices. Not long ago my five-year-old daughter, Lindsay, announced that she knew what the letters "s-a-y" spelled. Since she had been exposed to a wide variety of children's literature, I expected she would give the correct answer. Instead she replied that "s-a-y" spelled "zee". When I asked how she came to that conclusion, she said, "Well, the 's-a-y' at the end of 'Lindsay" says 'zee'." Her response revealed much more than the absence of "say" as a sight word. She was clearly noticing features of familiar words, generating hypotheses about sound/symbol relationships and word segments, and trying to apply these hypotheses to new words.

Physical Problems Which May Contribute to Spelling Difficulties

A conversation with a student may reveal information about physical problems which are not immediately apparent but which may have a significant impact on the child's spelling development. A child, for example, who is prone to ear infections in the primary grades may experience a hearing loss at a time when most children are highly sensitive to the relationship between sounds and letters. Even if the hearing loss disappears in later years, its presence at such a critical time may leave significant gaps in the child's understanding of the spelling system. The grade eight student whose spelling errors are shown below suffered hearing problems in childhood which left her with a mild hearing loss. Her spelling difficulties are characterized by problems with short vowels, consonant blends, incorrect final sounds, and word substitutions. Such errors are usually characteristic of much younger children.

Key Word	Student's Attempt
upset	upsat
thrown	throw
brushed	bushed
planet	planted
problem	promblem

3. The Child's Spelling Should Be Analyzed within a Developmental Framework

Many diagnostic spelling tools in the past encouraged teachers and their students to classify spelling errors on the basis of specific letter patterns such as inversions, substitutions, transpositions, and omissions. While such procedures call attention to the incorrectly spelled features of words, they support a narrow perceptual orientation to spelling acquisition. The spelling of *street* as *stret* is labeled an omission, whereas *streat* is a substitution.

What is absent from such classification schemes is an assessment of the child's current understanding of the spelling system. In the diagnostic framework described above, the two misspellings of *street* are seen as simply different error types. They may, however, represent two distinct stages in spelling development. The child who consistently spells long vowels with a single letter whose name "says" the sound is most likely at the "Letter Name" stage of development. Such a child is likely to spell *boat* as *bot*, *name* as *nam*, and so forth. Another child, who spells the same two words as *bote* and *naim*, is in the "Transition" stage of spelling development. These distinctions are not merely descriptive, but represent quite different hypotheses about written English. In the Letter Name stage, children assume a one-to-one correspondence between the sounds of English and specific letters. Therefore, they do not tend to experiment with vowel combinations, double consonants, silent letters, and the like. The Transition stage signals a more sophisticated understanding of the spelling system. Children at this stage are able to supplement simple sound/symbol correspondences with the realization that specific sounds are sometimes represented by more than one letter, as in vowel combinations and double consonants, and that the same sound may be spelled in a variety of ways. Zutell (1980) argues that the Transition stage of spelling development involves significantly more abstract concepts about language than previous stages. Therefore, while *bot* and *bote* are each spelled incorrectly, the differences they signal with respect to the learner must be addressed.

Similar distinctions can also be made with the spelling of older students. Research in the past decade (Henderson, 1985; Schlagel, 1982; Templeton, 1980) has revealed that children continue to form increasingly sophisticated hypotheses about written English throughout their high school and college years. Consider the spelling attempts of Students A and B below:

Key Word	Student A	Student B
invitation	invatashun	invitasion
knowledge	nollege	knowlegde

On a spelling dictation, both students would be judged as equally poor spellers. An examination of the "quality" of their errors, however, shows a more abstract understanding of the spelling system on the part of Student B. Student A seems to spell using a phonetic approach. The suffix *-ation* is simply spelled as it sounds. The spelling of *knowledge* as *nollege* is either generated phonetically or by analogy to a word such as *college*. Student B, however, is aware that the /shun/ portion of *invitation* is a suffix, and simply chooses the incorrect version. Student B uses another strategy characteristic of more mature spellers. In both words, an attempt is made to use the base word as a clue to spelling the related form. In the case of *knowledge*, the student is obviously aware that the base word is *know*. The schwa vowel in *invitation* is spelled correctly by referring to the base word *invite* in which the letter *i* is sounded. By looking at children's spelling errors within a developmental framework, you can make more appropriate decisions about instruction than by grouping on the basis of test scores.

4. Spelling Assessments Should Be Conducted over a Period of Time Using a Variety of Information Sources

The developmental framework for assessing growth in spelling focuses on the child's progressive understanding of the spelling system over time. It is important, therefore, to develop mechanisms for tracking the child's growth throughout the year. Orysia Hull (1989) suggests that the child's writing folder is an excellent vehicle through which progress in spelling can be observed. She describes a procedure in which the teacher keeps a copy of every piece of writing from every child early in the school year. One piece is then selected for each student as a basis for observing spelling growth. In the middle and again near the end of the school year, the original piece is dictated back to each student. Since the same words are involved in each instance, the quality of the child's spelling attempts can be traced over the three periods. This strategy also provides concrete information to use in discussing a child's progress in spelling during conversations with parents.

There is some danger, however, in basing a spelling assessment strictly on the child's personal writing. Many students learn to use in their writing only those words they are certain of spelling correctly. Their drafts may be virtually error-free, yet there may be many spelling principles which they have not grasped.

Furthermore, a child may be functioning well in a particular stage of spelling development which suits the current vocabulary level of the child's personal writing. It would be tempting for the teacher to decide that such a child needs no further assistance in spelling. In reality, however, the child may benefit from intervention which encourages movement to a more sophisticated stage of spelling development with its accompanying spelling patterns and vocabulary. Such is often the case with students in grades four to six who are proficient at spelling words of one or two syllables and are rated as competent spellers on the basis of their personal writing. When they begin to encounter more complex vocabulary in their reading, they suddenly face a large number of spelling principles which need to be addressed. These new words are not simply longer, but often require a more abstract understanding of the spelling system including the relationship between base words and derived forms, rules for adding prefixes and suffixes, words which are related in meaning, and Greek and Latin roots, to name but a few. Such children and their parents are often shocked and confused when the "competent speller" of previous years is suddenly faced with many spelling errors. Teachers, therefore, must look beyond a single source of information in determining a child's needs in the area of spelling.

Words dictated in the context of meaningful sentences also have a place in spelling assessment, since they often force children to attempt words they would not spell if they were choosing only familiar words for their writing. The teacher is then able to observe how the child approaches the task of spelling unfamiliar words. Some children will use a strictly phonetic approach; others will refer to a familiar analogous word such as *sight* for the spelling of *fright*; still others may give up in frustration and use only initial letters or substitute a completely different word. The use of a pretest before the students have an opportunity to study the words will often provide the most useful information concerning spelling strategies.

In *Spel . . . Is a Four-Letter Word*, Richard Gentry reveals that he is not a good speller despite having won awards for spelling in elementary school. He recalls writing two hundred and fifty-two perfect spelling tests and placing third in the county spelling bee, leading to a description of him in the local newspaper as one of the county's best spellers. In college, however, he was chastized by an English professor for producing "the worst example of a college student's spelling I've seen in five years of teaching."

The conflicting descriptions of Gentry's ability as a speller highlight a key principle in the assessment of spelling. When only one source of information is used, whether it be dictated spelling tests or personal writing, a true picture of the child's spelling skills is unlikely to emerge.

5. Spelling Assessment Should Lead to Appropriate Instruction

When spelling assessment focuses on what a child does know about the spelling system within a developmental framework, logical instruction goals become more readily apparent. Individual assistance may be provided to help a student consolidate a concept or move to a more sophisticated understanding of the spelling system. Several students may benefit from instruction concerning a spelling pattern or spelling strategies. There may be general concepts which the entire class can examine and discuss with the teacher. Resources, which may include spelling texts, can be used to respond to the needs described above. The starting point, however, should always be in the child's needs, rather than a prescribed set of skills predetermined by the teacher, a curriculum document, or the scope and sequence of a text. The child's needs and the skills anticipated by curriculum writers and authors of spelling texts may be surprisingly congruent if the knowledge derived from research on the developmental nature of spelling is incorporated into these materials. The teacher should, therefore, select resources with care.

Making the vital link between spelling assessment and instructional practices is a demanding task. A basic knowledge of both linguistics and the nature of learning to spell must be combined with sound instructional strategies and keen observational skills. Teachers will benefit from ongoing professional reading in these areas as well as frequent interaction with other colleagues in the examination of student writing and the sharing of experiences. The most productive source of information, is, as always, the students themselves. When children perceive that their teacher is trying to understand their individual needs rather than sorting and classifying for administrative purposes, assessment becomes truly collaborative. This sense of mutual learning and active involvement can then be carried over into spelling instruction. A natural link is formed between ongoing assessment and classroom activities, with the child placed in the only appropriate location — the centre.

Selected References

Buchanan, E. (1989). *Spelling for whole language classrooms.* Winnipeg: Whole Language Associates.

Gentry, R. (1987). *Spel ... is a four-letter word*. Toronto: Scholastic.

Goodman, K., Y. Goodman, and W. Hood (Eds.) (1989). *The whole language evaluation book*. Toronto: Irwin.

Henderson, E. (1985). *Teaching spelling*. Boston: Houghton Mifflin.

Hull, O. (1989). "Evaluation: the conventions of writing." In K. Goodman, Y. Goodman, and W. Hood (Eds.), *The whole language evaluation book*. Toronto: Irwin.

Schlagel, R. (1982). "A qualitative inventory of word knowledge: a developmental study of spelling, grades one through six." *Dissertation Abstracts International*, 47 (03), 915A. (University Microfilms No. 86-11, 798.)

Scibior, O. (1987). "Reconsidering spelling development: a socio-psycholinguistic perspective." *Dissertation Abstracts International*, 48 (07), 1720A. (University Microfilms No. 87-22, 916)

Scott, R. (1987). "Lessons in spelling." *Orbit*, 18 (3), 10-14.

Tarasoff, M. (1990). *Spelling strategies you can teach*. Victoria: Pixelart Graphics.

Templeton, S. (1980). "Spelling, phonology, and the older student." In E. Henderson and J. Beers (Eds.), *Developmental and cognitive aspects of learning to spell*. Newark: International Reading Association.

Zutell, J. (1980). "Children's spelling strategies and their cognitive development." In *Developmental and cognitive aspects of learning to spell*. Newark: International Reading Association.

PART VI

Beyond School

The media often use spelling assessment as a means of judging the efficacy of the school system, with little regard for the implications of these statistical surveys. And yet, in the community, spelling does count, and we must prepare students for a life of writing and rewriting. Sharon Siamon is a parent, and she chronicles her daughter Becky's growth in spelling. Storyteller Bob Barton brings us back to the wholeness of the words we love — spelling sense and taste — and nudges us into a love of language. His paper is a fitting end to this book.

Five Years in Transition: Profile of an Invented Speller

Sharon Siamon

Although Becky became a fluent writer at age six, using invented spelling, it was not until her eleventh year, in grade five, that her spelling began to approximate an adult standard. Looking back over her writing during a five-year period, I think that she reached a plateau at the transitional stage of development, and needed to develop personal strategies for individual word study in order to move forward.

When Becky began to write, between senior kindergarten and grade one, I noticed three things. First, because she had been encouraged to think of herself as a writer at home and at school, writing came naturally. She wrote messages, songs, and stories. She played school endlessly, writing activities for her "students", and comments on her own creative work. She wrote lists of things to do, people she liked, and words she knew how to spell. Already, at six, she perceived writing as a source of pleasure and a powerful tool. Fortunately, somewhere along the line she developed a passion for dating her writing, so that it is easy to follow her progress through the ensuing years.

Second, even at six, Becky used an array of spelling strategies to get control of this writing tool, from writing words such as *love* and *I* which she knew by sight to simple sound/symbol associations such as *mp* for *map*. She also copied words she knew how to read, such as *Jill* and *Sandy*, from old readers and *stop* and *exit* from signs. Although she was still grappling with such fundamentals as writing letters and numbers the right way around, and writing from left to right and top to bottom, she was developing a sense of word boundaries and sometimes indicated them by dots. And, when she wanted to write like an adult (as in filling in a cheque, or sticking a gummed message from "the teacher" on a piece of work), she still used scribble writing.

Third, and most important, Becky's growing sense of story and story language was not impeded by her inability to spell, and a phrase such as "Once upon a time" was used with confidence, even though it was spelled UNS.A.PON.A.TAM. This confidence grew as she wrote, so that by age seven she was writing story sentences such as *She also loved to wander in the field*. As a former primary teacher and mother of two older daughters, I knew what a breakthrough this represented in our attitudes toward writing and spelling. My other daughters seldom wrote for fun at home, as Becky did. If either of them had left a note in the bathroom such as this:

DO NAt Put The Brash anywar. Thank you.
by Becky Siamon

some family member would have been almost certain to point out their spelling errors. And as a teacher, I remembered spelling endless words on charts and boards so my students could write. There was an unspoken but well understood assumption that you didn't write what you couldn't spell. You asked, you looked it up, you copied from a friend, but you didn't just try it yourself! It was clear to see that Becky's teachers were enthusiastically embracing invented spelling, and encouraging creativity. Many of us, parents and educators, had a new consciousness about the way in which the development of children's written language paralleled the way infants and toddlers learn to speak — progressing naturally from one stage to another.

However, over the next four years, we began to lose our confidence in this "natural" progression. As Becky reached a transitional stage in her spelling she tried to approximate the patterns of written language she saw around her. Her spelling seemed to become more confused and inconsistent, and just as a young child will overgeneralize the "ed" endings on verbs and say "hitted" or "losted", so Becky would throw silent *e*'s on the end of every other word, and sprinkle double consonants generously here and there. Her spelling was not developing in a vacuum, but was influenced by a variety of factors, at home and at school.

For example, in March 1986, on her seventh birthday, Becky received a blue hardcover notebook, labelled *Stories by Becky Siamon*, from an adult friend. This seemed a great stimulus to do her very best writing, and has been kept safely in a special place in Becky's bedroom. The first story, written at seven years, one month, was about her birthday party and included the following:

> I got lase aiv prasinse. My purty was fun wane my sisactr
> pllayed gams wath me. I liked my purty

> (I got lots of presents. My party was fun when my sister
> played games with me. I liked my party)

A month later, in April, her topic was the night. The spelling of the title was corrected from *nate* to *night*, probably as the result of asking an adult.

At Night
> At nate I can her the wand bllw and the rane fall on the
> rafe.
> I lisine to puypple daine sars. I laie in bad and soon fall
> a slepe. I like the nate.

> (At night I can hear the wind blow and the rain fall on the
> roof. I listen to people downstairs. I lie in bed and soon
> fall asleep. I like the night.)

Obviously, her class had been working on an "I Like" theme. The next "story" was about her beloved friend Jody, whom she had been missing since our move to Toronto two years before.

My Fraude
> My fraude is Jaody. She is 8 earse old. She livds in Krllind-
> lake. She uosto lave be saed me. Hre eaeys are bulle. Hre

hare is blake. Hre skin is wiat. I like Joady.

(My friend is Jody. She is 8 years old. She lives in Kirkland Lake. She used to live beside me. Her eyes are blue. Her hair is black. Her skin is white. I like Jody.)

What interested me about the spelling was the way the sound/symbol associations seemed to be drifting off course as Becky experimented with her new awareness of patterns in English spelling — silent letters, vowel and consonant combinations — *Joady* for *Jody*; *blake* for *black*, *bulle* or *bllw* for *blue*. Sometimes this results in a logical spelling, as in *hare* for *hair* or *slepe* for *sleep*; at other times, as in *fraude*, it seems to be further from a phonetic matching. It appeared that Becky had reached the "transitional" stage of spelling development.

She was being careful not to make mistakes in this special writing book. The printing was her best. Her capitals and periods were carefully placed, and about one in four words had been erased and tried again (*bay* was erased and *be* substituted, for example). But it was hard not to be disappointed by the change in style and tone from the free-wheeling six-year-old. Becky's personal writing had clearly been influenced by the repetition and short jerky sentences of early reading instructional material. (As had her oral reading — at home she would often read aloud in the high-pitched halting monotone of the round robin reading class, instead of in her natural reading style, which was smoother and full of expression.)

Fortunately, somewhere between grades one and two, Becky stopped imitating the language of an old-fashioned pre-primer and recovered her written and oral fluency. At the same time, she was clearly expanding the number of high-utility words she knew how to spell, as she read and wrote regularly. In September of grade two, at seven years, six months, she wrote (at home) about the "Kilometre Club":

"The Callamtr Kallb"

The Callamtr Kallb is no ordnarary kallb. It hapes awre school to have hathryr chigine in awry Camynt. You mat ran a 100 times for your wahat stakr. You mat ran 200 foramadallean. you mat ran 205 for your wahat stakr madallean and Tsrt.

(The Kilometre Club is no ordinary club. It helps our school to have healthier children in our community. You must run a hundred times for your white sticker. You must run 200 for a medallion. You must run 205 for your white sticker, medallion and tee shrt.)

School on this draft was originally spelled with an *e* on the end, but that was self-corrected as she wrote. Becky could also spell *have, times, your*, and other one-syllable words without difficulty. But although her spelling "sight" list was growing, she was still using a mixture of strategies — writing single letters for whole syllables, as in *camy-n-t*; and using vowel placeholders, as in *mat* for "must". When she wanted a new word, she invented it with verve and confidence. *Los ove amachashne — soprb!* she wrote as a comment on a drawing during a game of school.

By Decenber 1986, still seven, and in grade two, she was writing poetry in her story book. Again, many of the words are erased and rewritten, and she has gone back and added an *e* to *there* on two occasions.

Thursday, Dec. 5, 1986 (I maed it up)
    "The Sunsat"
The sunsat is up. All clers are bite.
Bule, Prpell, Daerk Prpell, and white.
Pike and red,
All the clere are there. And if
you lookit one
deke nate, you
woed swaer. All
lose clers mite
be there.

(The sunset is up.
All colours are bright
Blue, Purple, Dark Purple, and white.
Pink and red.
All the colours are there
And if you look one dark night, you would swear.
All those colours might be there.)

Even though Becky had been exposed to the word *blue* for three and a half years in school, it was still giving her difficulty, although all the letters are there. "Dark" is spelled *daerk* and *deke* even though the pattern of *bark, dark, park, mark*, etc. is fairly common.

The following Thanksgiving, she was eight years and seven months old, in grade three, and following a traditional spelling program at school. After Thanksgiving, she wrote this entry in her blue story book:

By Becky Oct 13 Tuesday 1987
Ttaksgiving
At thaksgiving 18 pepele wir their. We Played baseball, socer, foteball, and dagj ball. Me and linsy writed a story on the canputer.

It is interesting to note that the spelling program was already having an effect, as evidenced by the confusion of *their* with *there*, or the spelling of *writed*.

As grade three went on, Becky continued to write at home in a variety of genres: plays, "published" books, notes, and lists for her own use such as this one.

Berash My hire.
Wash my hire.
Brash my teeth
Clene the rest of my room.
rede a capter of my Book.
Clen out my cost
call Jill at 11.30 and say to go home at 3.00.
Clen out Dechwasher
   things I Do Today

She was still comfortable using writing for a wide variety of purposes, even though her spelling remained inconsistent, and sometimes wildly inventive.

In grade four, with an excellent teacher, Becky continued to develop fluency. This matched a new thoughtfulness in her writing. In this example from her reading log she writes about the novel *The Midnight Fox*, by Betsy Byars:

Mar 9 The Midnight fox (pages) 42-48 F - novel
Today I really got into my book but I find if I stop reading its hard to start reading again. Most people think a book is two pecies of of cardbed with pages with words on them but this book *The Midnight fox* is more than that. It really exsites you. I recamend this book to all the people in this class. (so far)

The teacher, Donnalene Dalrymple, didn't correct the spelling in the reading log, but instead provided samples of correct writing of her own in response to the children's comments.

> Jan 24 — Becky — What a pleasure it is for me to step inside your "reading mind" for a few minutes as I enjoy your daily log. You are a reader that jumps, with both feet, inside a book. Your comments show that you are there, in the situations the characters find themselves in.

Although there was no formal spelling program in grade four there was a very active creative writing program throughout the year. Looking through Becky's notebooks and personal writing in this year it is easy to see the growth in command of the language — not so easy to see spelling growth. However, some samples are much better than others, which may suggest that Becky had good days and bad, and on the best days was beginning to move towards an adult model. As a parent, I was frankly beginning to wonder when that might happen.

As she turned ten, Becky was becoming more self-conscious about her spelling — at least partly because she was aware of our concern. She would often offer to read aloud something she had written, rather than have someone else read it — or make comments such as "Here's my story — but you probably won't be able to read it because of the spelling."

In the summer between grades four and five, however, two things happened which had a major impact on Becky's development as a mature speller. The first was her discovery that she could play "Family Feud" and "Jeopardy" on our home computer. The game was set up so that the children played against the machine. Becky soon learned that her ability to guess the correct words and "win" far exceeded her ability to spell the words correctly. And the computer was brutal. It didn't recognize *cost* or even *closit* as "closet". It didn't fill in missing letters or untangle misplaced ones. The computer in its simple-minded yes-or-no fashion simply didn't register close approximations as the same words.

The computer sat in a central area of our house, and as the game progressed we were treated to shrieks of "Oh No! Look! It was supposed to be a *g*, not a *j*." The game format presented the correct words (or spellings) at the end, so that the children could see how they were supposed to appear. Becky played word games for hours that summer, by herself, and with friends, and perhaps for the first time had a personal motivation for precision in spelling. The important thing about the computer was that though it offered plenty of incentives to be a good speller, it was non-judgmental about mistakes.

The second thing that happened was a chat I had with Ruth Scott about her doctoral thesis in spelling. She had found, she told me, that children who were good readers but poor spellers often lacked "word sense" — the idea of words as things in themselves, separate from their context. One of the ways this lack manifested itself was in the child's inability to generate and spell nonsense syllables. In other words, if I say "scram" to you, you will likely know how to spell other words that end with the same sound, such as *wham*, or *clam*; and can make up words that follow the same pattern, such as *plam*.

I thought that Becky, with her well-developed oral sense of rhyme, would have no trouble with nonsense syllables. I was wrong. She had trouble, at ten and a half, making the step from *jump* to *stump*, let alone the leap to a nonsense word like *glump*. But she soon warmed to the game and we played it often that summer. At the same time, I showed her how to look for small words in big ones — for the *break* and *fast* in *breakfast* — and we talked about why we "break" the "fast" at the beginning of the day.

It occurred to me that there might be a parallel between Becky's excellent reading comprehension, and her hesitant oral reading. Although she loved to read, reading aloud was not something she enjoyed. She would often skip small words, read *then* for *that*, or make other small miscues. She complained that reading out loud made it hard to understand what was happening. I wondered whether she was so focused on meaning that she was missing the individual words. Although this makes for efficient reading, as a writer I know that sensitivity to words is not just a matter of mechanics. Word study, for its own sake, is essential to writing well, and even essential to the pleasure of reading. Each word trails its own cloud of associations, history, aural and even visual impact.

One of the great pleasures of working with my daughter on words has been to watch Becky's sense of delight in words catch up to, and then surpass, my own. She understands for example, how *dab* is different than *bit*, if you're describing a small patch of colour in a sunset. Just recently she told me she has a list of favourite words, which includes "frothy", "crisp", and "rendezvous". She is interested in how these are spelled, because she loves their sounds.

As Becky entered grade five her ability to spell began to match her desire to write. In her autobiography Becky prepared a collage of meaningful images, and included the word "togetherness". This, she explained in an accompanying document, had to do with spelling:

> The word TOGETHERNESS is there because it reminds me of when my Mom taught me to look for small words in big words. In the word TOGETHERNESS the little words are to, get, her, and ness.

Becky's grade five teacher ran an individualized spelling program which seemed to suit Becky's style. Each week, she chose her own list of sixteen words, studied them, wrote sentences with them, and was tested on Friday. This is a sample list from November.

collecting	house	medieval	charge
giraffe	personal	music	flower
neighbour	mystery	horse	flags
want	English	humorous	detective

And a sample sentence: *In the* medieval *times the* English *were in* charge.

Knowing Becky's spelling history, many of her choices made good sense. *House* and *horse*, for example, were two words she had often mixed up, and *want* had been confused with *when* and *went*. *Giraffe* was one of the killer words from "Family Feud". *Detective* was a word for which she had tried several invented spellings on badges, door signs, reports, and stories. Playing detective had long been a favourite game. And *medieval* had been on her "how to spell?" list since a drawing she had made of a slinky black dress titled *"Modren Mid Evil"* had evoked laughter.

Although Becky's new attention to words and their spellings was having an effect on her writing, there was still much ground to cover. The final entry in the blue story book (to date) is this from midway through grade five:

> Becky Siamon Sun. Dec. 1989 30 New year's Eve
> For Christmas my favorite gift was from my Mom and Dad. It was a porcalain doll. I named he Anastagia, She has lether shoes with tacle laces. She has a pink pidaswa dress with

puffy sleves lace around the coaller that goes down about an inch (4 cm). Her hair is a *light* red and she has deep brown eyes like me. She has a pink podaswa bow in her hair too with dobble layers. She is beautiful. She has a posalian head, and hands up to the elbow, posalian feet up to the knees too. She is defitly my favorite gift of all!

Once again, three things were obvious. First, Becky's thirst for the experimental — reaching for words without much regard for correctness — had fortunately not been quenched. "Peau-de-soie" is not part of the average ten-year-old's spelling repertoire. Secondly, in the four and a half years since she began to write, Becky had developed an extensive vocabulary of most commonly used words, and words such as *beautiful, hair, eyes,* and *then* were spelled correctly, if not without some erasures. Thirdly, Becky is having trouble with words with less common patterns — words such as *leather, collar, double,* and *sleeves.* As she reached for words such as *porcelain* and *peau-de-soie,* when and how would she learn to spell *sleeve*?

One of the things I could do as a parent was to talk about these patterns whenever the subject of spelling came up. For example, when Becky asked for help making up her weekly spelling lists, I would try to extend patterns from words she had spelled before, such as *crazier* from *crazy,* or *designer* from *sign.* We also talked about how the spelling of root words influences the branches, as in *signal* and *sign.* In her grade five writing both at home and at school between New Year's and June, there was a steady growth in spelling awareness. For example, she saw information about an upcoming trip to Sweden lying around the house, and remarked that *komfort* and *klock-radio* were misspelled in the literature. When we pointed out that these words were the same in Swedish, but spelled slightly differently, she was interested. Even a year before, I don't think she would have noticed that they were spelled "wrong".

By summer 1990, at the age of eleven, Becky seems to have made the transition to an adult spelling model. In this sample from a journal, she records some sentences she wants to remember — perhaps they will appear someday in a finished piece of writing.

Book Sentences By Becky
1. In a Forest thicker then an old man's eyebrow. . .
   Made: Summer of 1987 age 8 on the way to Maine

2. There was a dab of sunset in the sky.
   Made: May 1 1990 on the way back from Brandy Lake
3. The grass was crispy to the touch from the fresh rain.
   Made: May 7 1990 looking out the window on a rainy
   day — staying home because sick.
4. The house was so old and dilapitated thet there was a
   rusty fog around it
   Made: Thought of in a dream (nightmare) In Hotel June
   8 1990

My daughter's development as a mature speller depended on many things. It depended on her strong desire to communicate in written language. It depended on having the adults and other children in her life provide models of writing: lists, notes, manuscripts, and teacher communications. It depended on her reading a broad range of materials at home and at school. Somewhere along the line it depended on an awareness of standards and the importance of precision in spelling — to win a game, to avoid being laughed at, to communicate clearly. All of these factors provided her with reasons to want to spell well. Although the strategies for early spelling development seemed to come naturally, the final transition to correct spelling was a more conscious development of strategies such as individual word study.

In the interview that follows, Becky has the last word. She talks about her problems in learning to spell, and the strategies she has used to overcome them. She's aware of the limitations of a strategy such as using the sound of the words, and the appropriateness of strategies such as the dictionary or computer spell check. In the end, she concludes, it all comes down to practice.

S: What do you remember about learning to spell?

B: I remember that it was harder than other subjects, and the English language didn't make any sense — things like *fridge*, which should be spelled *frig*.

S: When did you first start thinking about spelling as different than writing?

B: When I was in grade three. We had spelling tests every week, a trial on Thursday and a final on Friday, and the rest of the week we studied the words by writing out sentences and writing them over a whole bunch of times. Every time you got a final test right a coloured sticker went up on the board in front of the whole class. The person with the most stickers at the end of the year got to go with the teacher to McDonald's.

S: Was that you?

B: No, it was Randy — he was smart in every subject, except for math.

S: What has helped you most to learn how to spell?

B: Video games on the computer like "Family Feud" and "Jeopardy".

S: Why?

B: Because, if you don't spell it right, you don't get the answer right, and you don't get the points. They print the correct answer out on the screen after you get it wrong.

S: So you remember it for next time?

B: Yeah. Sometimes they have the questions repeated, so you're prepared.

S: What else has helped you learn to spell?

B: School, I guess, because if you don't get your spelling right you get marks taken off your work.

S: That's why you want to spell correctly, but what helps you do it?

B: Just jotting things down once in a while, you sort of figure it's wrong by looking at it. If it's a longer word you can pick out the parts. If it's a short word and the spelling doesn't make any sense, it's still hard to spell. I'm better at spelling long words than short ones.

S: Do you think about spelling when you're writing a story?

B: No, not usually. But if I know a word I sit and think about it for a while, but if I don't know it I just go on.

S: Do you ever look words up in the dictionary?

B: Yes. Usually, if you look words up in the dictionary, you're doing a good copy of something. You wouldn't do it for something private.

S: Do you use the spell check on the computer?

B: Yes, at the end of things.

S: Does it help?

B: Well, it doesn't teach you how to spell things, but it does help if you're in a hurry.

S: How would you help teach someone to spell?

B: Teach them how to pick out parts of words, like "to-get-her".

S: How about the sound of words? Does that help you?

B: Yes it does, but not always, because some of the words are really weird. I use sound a lot, but I usually get the word wrong. For example, when I was playing "Family Feud" and I had to spell North Carolina, I spelled it *North Care a line a*, which makes a lot more sense than Carolina!

S: How did you know how to spell North, for example?

B: Well, after you learn that the "th" sound is *th*, you can sound out the *nor*. The older you are, the more you know how to spell, not because you're smarter or anything, but because you've done it so often.

A Storyteller Comments: Highway Relish

Bob Barton

Each autumn, my mother carts home from the Hamilton Farmers' Market the fruits of the rich Ontario harvest, which quickly find their way into the various relishes and chili sauce which she puts down. She has done this most of her life and we reap the benefits each time she comes to visit with carefully wrapped jars in the bottom of her canvas shopping bag.

One of her specialties is a mustard and pickle-type mixture which she calls "Highway Relish". It is probably a kind of piccalilli or chow chow, and somewhere in time was known by a different name. My mother inherited this recipe from her aunts in Paris, Ontario and the story goes that they obtained it from a lady who lived out along the highway — hence the name "Highway Relish".

I guess everyone can cite examples such as this from their own hoard of family stories, but it is just this kind of anecdote which stimulates us to think of words as personalities with their own stories, indeed histories.

As an eight-year-old I was fascinated by an incident in our class reader. I credit this moment with helping raise my consciousness about words and the notion that every word is a story. A spelling bee was featured in a story and during the tense closing moments, when all but one speller had been eliminated from each side, the word which broke the tie was "separate". The loser spelled it *seperate*. The winner, who had been coached by a grandparent, had been taught to find words inside a word and to make up a story about the parts. For her, *separate* represented a little tale about "a rat named Sep". I thought the idea brilliant at the time and thereafter came to think of words in terms of their stories, the ones that travel with them, like "Highway Relish" and "separate" and the ones that I later invented.

I believe that it was this association of word and story which caused me to seek in the books that I was reading unusual words that set my mind spinning and to store them away for later use. After all these years I still carry around in my wordhoard "bumbershoot" (meaning umbrella, from a Bobbsie Twins adventure), "heffalump" from *Winnie-The-Pooh*, and the wonderful names of the animals from Kipling's *Jungle Book* — Mowgli, Shere Khan, Baloo, to mention a few. Poetry also stimulated my interest in wordstory. Is there a more dynamic way you can witness words at work? I know my preschool experiences with the Randolph Caldecott illustrated nursery rhymes and continual revisiting of *Johnny Crow's Garden* opened my eyes and ears to the world of words.

I don't necessarily hold with those who consider spelling to be next to godliness, but I do believe that a word's spelling is important in that it is an aspect of that word's personality as surely as its sound, its meaning, and its story. For this reason, throughout my career I have gone out of my way to cultivate in students an interest in words because I believe that if you come to care about them you will pay attention to them, and this in turn will go a long way towards encouraging an interest in their structure as well as their sound and meaning.

English spellings can be tricky. Some words sound the same but look different or look the same but sound different. Some even look and sound the same but have entirely different meanings depending on their use. All of this can be pretty daunting for some children. It is for this reason that I like them to be bold with words and encourage them to play games with them. These games involve the children in manipulating shape, sound, meaning, and story in an effort to allow words to demonstrate their unique shapes and personalities.

Willard Espy's books *An Almanac of Words at Play* and *A Children's Almanac of Words at Play* have proved invaluable in stimulating my thinking about ways that words could be made worthy of time and attention. For example, a comment in Espy's introduction to *An Almanac of Words at Play* once sent the children and me scrambling to emulate it:

> *An Almanac of Words at Play* is something of a three-ring circus of words: words clowning; words walking tightropes; words venturing their heads into the mouths of lions; words cleaning up after the elephants.

From this statement we evolved a vocal jazz composition entitled "Flummery", which means the word at play. We gathered together all the words that described words playing; puns, anagrams, alliteration, tongue twisters, echolalia, palindromes, homophones, twosomes, and onomatopoeia. From this collection, a framework was built on which to hang the examples.

The composition opened with the choral spelling of "flummery", repeated three times with an accelerating speed in a manner resembling a steam engine pulling out of a station. Two alternating choruses then chanted back and forth their definitions of flummery. Side A chanted "fooling around words" and side B replied "words doing cartwheels". Four quartets each chorused three examples of words at play which they had arranged in pleasing sound patterns (e.g., palindrome, homophone, anagram, pun), then the entire group focused on the tongue twister "unique New York", which was spoken at a rapid pace ten times, increasing in volume and ending in a shout.

A soft chorus of words selected from the children's French vocabulary (tête à tête, pas de deux) formed a background for solo performances of palindromes such as "madam I'm Adam" and "rotor", "radar", and "eve".

The grand finale consisted of three onomatopoeic choruses rendering the sound of their chosen words — "fuchsia", "babble", and "pop" — as a vocal collage.

All of this activity involved the children in ransacking dictionaries and thesauruses, intense listening and looking activity, oral editing, the writing down of copious lists of words and participation in ongoing discussion and storying about words. But most important, the children were finding pleasure in it.

In building awareness of words, in making words truly memorable, I believe that they must be featured in circumstances which allow their true weight to shine. Robert McNeil has some interesting things to say about this in his book *Wordstruck*:

> In the torrents of words that drown our culture, have we forgotten how to listen? ... To get it "right" we turn increasingly to computers and smart typewriters. Yet the more we process words electronically, and let computer programs choose our vocabulary, spelling and syntax, the more disconnected we may become, the more remote from the sound of our language, and therefore from a feeling for the weight of words.

Ah yes, a feeling for the weight of words! Words heard, seen, investigated. Words sung, sounded, celebrated. Spelling for me must be seen within this greater context, this attempt to personalize, this attempt to see the story in words, of words, around words. James Hillman says it all for me:

> [Words] are personal presences which have whole mythologies: genders, genealogies (etymologies concerning origins and creations), histories and vogues; and their own guarding, blaspheming, creating and annihilating effects. For words are persons. . .

Publishing Acknowledgements

Some of the papers in this book were originally published as follows:

Gentry, J. Richard. "Developmental Aspects of Learning to Spell". *Academic Therapy*, 20:1, September 1984.

Henderson, Edmund H., and Shane Templeton. "A Developmental Perspective of Formal Spelling Instruction through Alphabet, Pattern, and Meaning". *The Elementary School Journal*, 86:3, 1976.

Preen, Judith. "A Whole Language Approach to Spelling". *Prime Areas*, 31:2, Winter 1989.